Shores & Falls

Virginia Mueller

Libra Chai

Copyright

Shores & Falls: Traveling Iceland's Ring Road
©2023 Virginia Mueller
All rights reserved. No part of this book may be reproduced or used in any manner without prior written permission except for usage protected under fair use. This includes selling and distributing copies on unapproved platforms.
Ebook ISBN: 978-1-7374921-6-0
Paperback ISBN: 978-1-7374921-8-4
Cover art photography by Virginia Mueller @2022

Printed by Libra Chai

Contents

1. Notes — 1
2. Pre-Trip Planning — 3
3. Arrival — 8
4. Food Lovers Tour — 14
5. Banking — 22
6. Maritime Museum — 25
7. Blue Lagoon — 32
8. Ring Tour Start! — 40
9. The Golden Circle — 42
10. South Coast Falls — 52
11. Feather River Canyon — 60
12. Falling Glacier — 64
13. Jökulsárlón Glacier Lagoon — 74

14.	Aurora Hunting	80
15.	Austurland	86
16.	The Hanging Falls	94
17.	Evening Searches	102
18.	Collapsing Waterfall	110
19.	Námaskarð & NASA	115
20.	Mývatn Baths	119
21.	Dark Castles	122
22.	Waterfall of the Gods	126
23.	Akureyri Storms	132
24.	Troll Peninsula	137
25.	Triplet Craters	146
26.	Lava Falls	151
27.	Snorri Sturluson	153
28.	Sturlureyki Horse Farm	158
29.	Hallgrímskirkja	163
30.	Reykjavik Night Life	168
31.	Departure	174
32.	Iceland Guide	178

Notes

This is primarily a travelogue of a nine-day trip to Iceland in September 2022 but may also serve as a guidebook covering Iceland's history and mythology. To that end, you'll find various resources in this book.

The first is a bunch of footnotes. This book is full of information learned from my tours and further research into the sights I saw upon my return. I encourage you to use them to discover more about anything that interests you – from Iceland's geographic history to NASA's training missions in the country. If anything catches your eye, please use them as a guide for further reading!

The other is a list of recommendations to help you plan your trip to Iceland and features a list of hotels, restaurants, tour companies, and sights. But to start, I highly recommend Arctic Adventures.[1] I've used them for a variety of excursions during both of my trips to Iceland.

---

1. Article Adventures, 2023 https://adventures.is/

In addition to the guides, I've structured this book first into days and then into attractions to provide an outline of a potential itinerary and offer an understanding of how much you can pack into a day.

***

As this is a travelogue recounting my adventures, names have been changed for privacy. Events and experiences are as I can recall them.

***

Where possible, I used the Icelandic spelling, including the use of two consonants absent from the English language. I did this in an effort to be as authentic as possible, but I understand they can get in the way of pronouncing these words. So here's a small guide.

The two characters, in upper case and lower case form, are Ð ð and Þ þ. Both make a 'th' sound, but placement can make a difference. Þ þ is primarily seen at the beginning of words and makes a 'th' like 'thunder' or 'theater'. Ð ð by contrast is only in the middle or end of words. In the middle it sounds like the 'th' in 'feather' or 'mother', but at the end in more like 'thin' or 'the'.

As an example, the geographical park where the continental divide rests is called Þingvellir. Many English guides spell it Thingvellier.

Pre-Trip Planning

I first visited Iceland in 2018.

It was a spontaneous trip. I'd just quit my job, I had a gap before starting my new one, and Google told me flights to Iceland were cheap and not that long. I put out a call on Facebook, a friend joined me from Budapest, and a week later I was enjoying coffee in Reykjavik. We had a delightful, if cheap, week in each other's company. We ate a lot of egg sandwiches made in the hostel kitchen.

It was a trip my mother was more than a little jealous of, and when we saw COVID-19 restrictions start to lift decided we'd plan a mother-daughter trip. As plans shifted, we each extended an invitation to a travel buddy. She brought Michele, an old friend from college. I brought Vikki, a friend I met through work.

Going a second time was no burden to me, I'd highly enjoyed my first trip. Yet, as it'd been a series of day trips from Reykjavik, there was a fair amount I'd left undone. My bucket list included doing the ring road - the state highway that circled the island - and seeing the aurora. My previous trip had been in late May when long sunlight hours made it impossible to see the night sky.

As the planning for this trip fell on me due to my familiarity, I made sure both items were on the itinerary. Wishlist items from my travel buddies – waterfalls, hikes, glaciers – were also added to our nine-day schedule. We bought tickets in June for a September trip, planning several days in the capital before taking off for a tour around Iceland.

Ultimately, the things we wanted to do on this trip were:

- Circle the country

- See the northern lights

- Gaze upon wild reindeer

- Waterfall hikes

- Hike a glacier

- Soak in geothermal spas

- Take in beautiful sea views

Google told us to prepare for cold, rainy weather. Layers would be a must, and I updated my hiking wardrobe before going. I should have gotten an REI membership after that first purchase; I would have recouped the fee in cashbacks before the year was up. Many of those purchases had been in the week prior to departure – inspired by a dinner Vikki and I had a week before we left where it became *very* obvious she'd not done any research.

"I'll need hiking shoes?"

"Yeah, for the crampons we'll need for the glacier hike. They don't work with regular gym shoes."

I dropped off a bag of items for her to try on and potentially pack the day before we left. Even then, the girl is last minute enough that she returned from a shopping trip 90 minutes before leaving for the airport.

Despite what felt like a scramble, we were all perfectly packed for the trip. I think there's only one shirt I didn't use. In typical me habit, I did bring more reading material than I needed. I knew two paperbacks and a kindle might be too much, but I did it anyway. At least I was in good company – we all expected to do more reading than we did.

Arrival

While we planned to leave out of O'Hare, only two of us lived in Chicago. Michele's husband, generous and with a lot of extra time, volunteered to drive her to O'Hare. No small thing, as she's three hours away on the west side of Michigan.

My mother is even farther, hailing from Detroit. She drove to Michele's house, then hopped in the car with Mr. Michele behind the wheel.

Michele and my mom met in medical school and have been friends roughly 30 years. They both work in emergency medicine, though Mom specializes in children, and bonded over classes and struggles. Mom immigrated from Greece - though at an early enough age her childhood experiences mirror those of first generations. Michele is an American-Filipino woman who clings to her culture strongly. I remember a family visit when I was ten where she forced her sons to showcase a traditional dance. They grumbled, but the performance was cool, the sound of stick hits bounced off dumbbells and a treadmill. The dance reminded me of jump rope games. It was so different from the Greek dancing I'd learned, where you hold hands and snake a single-file line.

Needless to say, I've known Michele my entire life. She and my mom were pregnancy partners, with each of their three kids born within months of each other. We have boxes of photos with the two of them both pregnant and us kids playing. I vaguely remember zoo trips with her boys. We no longer lived in the same area after I turned 5 or 6. As I got older, I saw Michele and her family less but as one of my mother's best friends she was never forgotten. I'd never gone on a trip with her, and it had been several years since we'd last seen each other. Mom sees her more regularly. In fact, they had a weekend planned two months after our return to the States.

Vikki and I haven't known each other nearly as long, only seven years. She immigrated in 2011, coming to the States for school, and never left. We're old coworkers still friends despite several job changes on both our ends. While not pregnancy partners, we're home partners, having gone through the hassle of real estate searches and mortgage lending the same season.

Despite our years of knowing each other, we'd never vacationed together. Not even a weekend getaway. Mom and Michele have traveled a few times as a pair, including to see me in New Zealand when I spent a semester abroad working at a marketing start-up. Mom and I frequently travel abroad together, most recently in 2018 to Greece.

Vikki and Michele had never met, and how we'd work as a travel unit was a mystery. There'd been a few fielded questions – Vikki asking about Michele, Michele hitting my mom up about Vikki. Were we looking for the same thing from the trip? Have an equal interest in hiking? Should we anticipate microaggressions? We'd be in each other's pockets, 24-hour contact, for over a week. They were all valid concerns, and I'll admit I was worried about being the odd introvert of the group.

While Vikki arrived at the airport separately, it was within the same five minutes. It was a sign – we were predestined travel buddies. It didn't help that Michele took one look at Vikki and jokingly declared them the second mother-daughter pair of the group. Vikki laughed, happy at the sudden inclusion, and indeed they had been considered as such at least once during the trip despite Michele's Filipino roots and Vikki's Mongolian ones.

We'd gotten to the airport very early; Mr. Michele had a three-hour return trip home and hadn't wanted to get caught in the dark. We went through security with no issues but were dismayed to find out we'd arrived so early we didn't have a gate assignment. We hefted our backpacks and started walking toward the terminal anyway.

O'Hare is an outdated airport. We transitioned between terminals via a tunnel lit with a neon light display hanging from the ceiling and paneled walls that reminded me of faded paint color strips. Outlets were hard to find, and the seats at the gate weren't attractive to sit in for hours. We parked in a food court, especially when we saw cocktails were only $12. That's a good price for a Loop bar, and to find it in an airport was a miracle. And they didn't skimp on the rum!

Chatting and catching up, the time passed quickly. For most of us, this was our first international trip since COVID, and we clutched our masks and kept space between us and other diners. I'd already gone through my re-introduction to travel last fall for a domestic trip, which had edged me the closest I've ever been to an anxiety attack.

While this trip wasn't as stressful, I still found myself very aware of every stranger around me. I also found myself oddly thankful for getting COVID months earlier. It might have ruined my Fourth of July weekend, but I was still in the three-month period of strong antibodies that would make reinfection unlikely. Vikki had suffered through it at the same time – though we'd not gotten it from each other – and my mother contracted COVID more recently less than a month before. Michele simply bragged about having one more booster shot than the rest of us.

This was the first time I had seen my mother since she'd caught COVID. I'd gone home to help care for her; I couldn't *not* when I heard how weak her voice had been on the phone. By the time I got there, she was recovered enough to not sleep the days away but watching her get winded by simple house chores was shocking.

We spent Labor Day weekend on opposite sides of the great room, reading our separate books, and the highlight of the weekend was when she felt well enough to learn how to order groceries online. We were both masked and in a room with windows open, but I was impressed she had the mental skills to learn. My own COVID brain fog didn't completely lift for three weeks, and Mom's case of stronger physical than mental symptoms had me concerned about her possibility of developing long COVID. But here she was, back to her old self as we traded cocktails and food around the table. It made me happy.

When it came time to fly, we were a rare group wearing K95 masks which I found irksome. But with regulations no longer requiring them, I was just glad I had an aisle seat and no neighbors. We managed to book a square, each of us on the aisle of subsequent rows, and the flight impressed me. There's a trend of higher cost and lower service, but our 6-hour United flight came with a blanket, a pillow, and two very tasty meals. Not bad for economy fare.

We left Chicago at 9:30 pm and landed at 8:30 am in Reykjavik. With a six-hour time difference, the plan was to push through the day until we dropped. To enforce it and keep us active, we had a tour scheduled at 11:30 that would serve as adrenaline, a city tour, and lunch.

The airport is an hour outside of the city. I'm so glad our taxi driver was chatty; he kept us awake by giving us small lessons on how to pronounce Icelandic words and what to see in the capital. For all that Iceland is a beautiful country, that road between the airport and Reykjavik is not. Rocky and treeless, which Michele noted reminded her of Hawai'i, the scenery was dark gray rocks, blue-grey ocean, and pale green lichen.

After checking into our hotel, we headed out in search of coffee. Immediately we ran across Iceland's high prices. After conversions, black coffee cost $5 and my mocha $8. While more expensive than most of my coffee shop runs, just the week before my grocery store Starbucks had charged me almost $7 for a tall PSL. I knew food would be expensive this trip, but I hoped if I curbed my need for upgrades I could keep costs manageable.

The café had good coffee, at least, and it was the perfect introduction to many of the restaurants we found ourselves in later that day – full of wooden, narrow spaces that reminded me of older New England homes that played oldie American music.

Caffeinated, we headed out into the drizzle. We walked down Laugavegur, loving the car-free nature of it and the variety of murals on the asphalt. Vikki and I linked arms to jump through a hopscotch 150 spaces long, then raced on a painted track. We were in a new city, on a much-needed vacation, and reveled in stretching our legs. We leaned on each other, giggling, as Michele and Mom caught up, the energy infectious. Even as the rain increased as we headed to our meet point at Ingolfur Square, we didn't care.

Vacation mode on.

Food Lovers Tour

By the time we got to Ingolfur Square, the rain picked up enough that I worried about my jeans soaking up the water. As my only pair, I didn't want them to become so soaked they wouldn't dry overnight.

I looked between the falling water and Vikki, huddled in her new coat. She looked back at me and rolled her eyes, but I saw the thanks in it. I was the reason she even considered packing rain gear, and here we were, using it our first three hours in Iceland.

Our tour guide was slightly late, but when she arrived the rain had let up enough we could pull down our hoods. The Reykjavik Food Lovers Tour was off!

Our first stop was Iðnó, a converted theater that kept the main space in good repair for banquets but had turned the other parts of the building into a cute bistro. We walked into a light-filled lobby dotted with white tables, then trooped upstairs. As we settled into our seats in a wide, sunny room, our guide talked about the country's history and its impact on cuisine.

In terms of native plants, there's not much. No native land animals worth consuming either. In fact, the arctic fox is Iceland's *only* native mammal. Iceland's biodiversity is limited, even compared with similar climates and geography like Scandinavia.

A big reason for this is that Iceland is geologically *young*. Young enough to not have any dinosaur fossils. Glaciers' recent, again by geological standards, coverage of the country reduced the opportunity for plants to grow and develop. There were also frequent volcano eruptions, which have a habit of wiping out vegetation and leaving behind hostile landscapes. On top of that, Iceland is an isolated island in cold waters. Land animals had a hard time migrating to the island. [1] All this means what settlers could eat on the island was limited to imported livestock and local fish. Transported livestock caused their own issues. The local plants were tasty and had little protection, leading to overgrazing that in turn let do soil erosion. And with poor soil, there was little chance for native flora to succeed. [2]

Early settlers also decimated local birch forests. Eventually, that lack of wood became an issue. Homes were constructed from sod, not wood, and a low supply of timber meant wood couldn't be used as a common fuel source. Many actions that required boiling water, like isolating salt or making tea or pasta, were rarely performed.

All this drastically restricted Icelanders' ability to develop local dishes. That doesn't mean they didn't though!

---

1. Icelandic Institute of Natural History. *Flora*. 2023 https://www.ni.is/en/flora-funga/flora

2. Wikipedia. *Wildlife of Iceland*. 2023 https://en.wikipedia.org/wiki/Wildlife_of_Iceland

Our meal started with unleavened flatbread, which our guide explained has historically been cooked in the earth thanks to Iceland's geothermal energy. It took longer but could bake unwatched. The bread was also made from rye, as the cold weather was kinder to it than wheat. I found the bread more flexible and softer than I expected, as well as heartier. Especially when coated with a spread of unsalted butter and smoked lamb.

Even as a Greek, I'd never eaten smoked lamb before, which I now know is a travesty.

Next up was a lamb stew, which plays the same role in Iceland as chicken noodle soup. Carrot bits, celery, potato, and meat chunks, but with a less salty broth. The soup used to be frequently made with mutton, as wool was so important as a trade good that sheep weren't bread for meat. Lamb was considered a delicacy.

Icelanders used to eat a fair amount of horse meat, but it was banned as the country converted to Christianity. Today, people do eat horse but it's rare as the animals aren't bred for the market.[3] I hoped to try some at some point during the trip, just to do it, but never got the opportunity.

Our next stop was a fish and chips place called 101 Reykjavik Street Food. I was excited, I'm constantly chasing the taste of a favorite fish and chips place in New Zealand. However, our tour guide ordered fish soup for the group. I'd hesitate to call it a soup, as it was white fish mixed with thin mashed potatoes. With it came a very dense rye bread, once again baked with earth heat, that included syrup as an

---

3. Your Friend in Reykjavik. *Horse Meat in Iceland.* 2023 https://yourfriendinreykjavik.com/horse-meat-in-iceland/

ingredient to sweeten it. I found myself delighting in the meal, helped by the cold, wet weather outside.

Pulling up our hoods, we wove through wet streets to our next location on the food tour. I couldn't help but stare, it was a hot dog stand, but our tour guide explained it's a city staple. Bæjarins Beztu Pylsur had been owned by the same family for 80 years, and it wasn't uncommon for long lines to develop during workdays. It's claim to fame was lamb hot dogs, another item Greek me can't believe I haven't had.

In terms of toppings, the hot dogs were similar to a Chicago dog - ketchup, mustard, two types of onions, and a relish. Despite being a Chicago lass, I've never been a fan of Chicago dogs. I asked for just ketchup.

"How boring," Mom teased as we tried to squeeze under the stand's awning. She might have been okay with getting rained on, but I wasn't.

Vikki joined me, passing over my hot dog. I stared at the naked dog, wondering if they'd forgotten my ketchup, but no. All toppings had been placed *under* the dog. I eagerly ate it, the warm food a balm in the damp air. It had a thicker casing than a beef dog, and while tasty I'll stick to beef hotdogs. That just feels right.

Vikki, poor thing, didn't even finish hers. "It's just okay," she said. "And this is our third meal and we're not done." I nodded. While we'd been served small portions so far, my stomach was full.

Our guide clapped her hands. "One last stop!" she called out, "it's a little bit of a walk, so stay close."

We scurried to follow her. The rain fell harder, from a drizzle to hard enough to feel each drop hit my raincoat. I flipped my gaze from the street to avoid puddles and our guide to making sure my party was close by. We walked along the harbor for a few blocks, and I started to shiver. The weather wasn't particularly cold, but with the wet, I was starting to feel it.

Eventually, we were shepherded into a small place called Seabaron. We hurried inside, up a set of glazed wooden stairs, and beelined for a set table. The walls were made of pale but thick wood beams, and above our table was mounted a grid of porcelain plates depicting blue multi-masted sailboats. I peeled my raincoat off and hung it on the back of a chair. "We'll be here for a while," our guide said. "What would you like to drink?"

I requested coffee just to have something to warm my hands and belly.

First item on the menu was a lobster tomato bisque, with a slight curry flavor to it. We slurped it up, grateful for the warmth and spice. It was so much better than Campbell's, and just what the group needed after the rain.

Next came shark, which has to undergo quite a process for safe consumption. As our tour guide explained, shark meat is toxic because they don't have a liver to filter their blood. Preparing the meat for consumption involves using gravity to press the toxins out of the shark before leaving it out to rot. Only then was it safe to eat.[4] As one person asked, how did someone even stumble across that process?

The shark was part of a combo, a one-two punch like tequila and lime. Eat the shark square, our guide told us, then down a shot

---

4. Your Friend in Reykjavik. *The Fermented Shark of Iceland.* 2023 https://yourfriendinreykjavik.com/fermented-shark-iceland/

of black death. A potato-based alcohol like vodka, black death is a strong, clear liquor flavored with caraway. It went down smoothly and the warmth traveled through my body *very* quickly. I'd channeled my college days, knocking the shot back as soon as I swallowed the shark, and regret it. I would have preferred to have the shark, which had a citric-acidic taste, linger in my mouth longer before it got burned away. Black death, in comparison, tasted like ouzo-light.

The star of the meal was whale. I hadn't known people ate it anymore, and I associate whale hunting with long-ago desires for oil. But Iceland still hunts whales, with sustainability safeguards such as only one company allowed to do it and species-specific quotas.[5] Minke whales have the larger quota and are what we were served. I honestly would have called it beef if I hadn't known it was whale, albeit very tender, dissolve-in-your-mouth beef. It goes through a tenderizing and marinating process that takes several days, but the taste is worth it.

The rain hadn't let up while we ate. We tramped through puddles up to the hotel, occasionally taking shelter in tourist shops. At the hotel, we lost Michele to the pull of sleep. She'd worked the overnight the day before our departure and had only dozed on the drive into Chicago and on the plane. I'm impressed she lasted so long, but I credit that to the tour keeping us moving and entertained for a few hours.

I knew if I stopped moving, I'd crash and ruin my sleep schedule. Vikki and Mom declared that it was time to shop and I trailed along.

---

5. Your Friend in Reykjavik. *Whale Meat in Iceland.* 2023 https://yourfriendinreykjavik.com/whale-meat-in-iceland/

The rain had let up, back to a drizzle that turned my curls to frizz. We went in and out of stores, ranging from the local version of Patagonia (Ice Wear) to artist galleries to jewelry stores to small boutiques. While the coffee that morning had been pricey, but not outrageous, I couldn't help but balk at the idea of 10,000 ISK (71 USD) for a wool knit hat. I'd have to bargain hunt for a souvenir or make sure it was worth it.

Eventually, I begged to sit. I love walking around and being outside, but if there is one thing I could change about my body it'd be my feet. Flat and wide, I'd never been good at prolonged periods of standing before they started to hurt. I'd rather hike five miles than browse a mall for an hour, the start and stop worse than constant movement. With all of us feeling the pull to rest, we slipped into a bar that felt punkish despite the close quarters and rich, old wood that many Reykjavik buildings contain. We sipped Irish Coffee in a corner booth, enjoying the diffuse light from the window and teaching Vikki how to play Rummy. Mom snickered every time she won – which was every hand but one.

Despite that being my third coffee of the day, I quickly sagged. I shuffled Vikki and Mom back toward the hotel. Knowing no one had the energy for dinner, we cruised through the only grocery store we'd seen to pick up snacks. Rye leavened bread. Smoked lamp cut like deli meat. Cheese. We had a relaxed evening in the hotel, trading time in the bathroom, holding warm mugs of orange tea, and listening to Michele chat through her second wave.

We would have all the next day to explore the capital city, but no one had the capacity to plan it. We slipped into bed, leaving tomorrow's plan building for the morning.

Banking

The day started with groans and a surprisingly light workout routine. While the beds had been comfy and large, even with two to a bed we didn't feel cramped, travel and strangeness meant we all woke up wanting a good stretch. I'm surprised we managed; the hotel room was a studio with side-by-side queens separated by a barely-there wall from a tight sitting area feet from the bathroom door and kitchenette. I braced my legs on the kitchen counter while I brushed my teeth, watching Vikki do planks in the sitting room while Mom touched her toes standing at the foot of the bed and Michele stood next to the window, stretching fingers to the ceiling.

Vikki was the most ambitious, getting in a light workout. Crunches, planks, push-ups. She'd been disappointed enough that none of our hotels would include gyms to the point she considered bringing weights. I'm glad she didn't pack dumbbells and made do with floor exercises. I was impressed and motivated, so did a bit of floor work until the itchy carpet and acute awareness of chair legs had me stop.

Mom praised our dedication as she stepped over Vikki to head to the bathroom.

For breakfast, we moseyed to a bakery our food guide called the best in Iceland - Baka Baka. A black wooden building on a corner of Laugavegur, one side of the building was composed of windows displaying racks and racks of flaky pastries. Baka Baka specializes in croissants, so we each ordered a different flavor – plus a few extra to share with the table. My favorite was the cardamon croissant, which kept teasing at the flavor of an apple tart without the stickiness, as well as the almond croissant that had been filled with a mild custard. Everything, however, was delicious: flakey, buttery, and warm. Thinking about them months later, I would eagerly buy a dozen right now.

I'd been eyeing the bank each time we walked by yesterday, so I led the group to it after we filled our stomachs. I was concerned that once we were on the ring road, there'd be situations where cash was preferred, or required, and there'd be no place to get it. Reykjavik, after all, is the largest city in Iceland and I'd seen only one grocery store and one bank.

The bank was old-fashioned in a neo-classical sense, with columns and marble floors, and some of the walls were topped by a narrow mural. They reminded me of Impressionist paintings, large and colorful showing historical scenes. Near the exchange desk was a more modern mural, a blocky depiction of the harbor that took up a whole wall. The bank also had a small gallery of abstract art it acquired in the 80s, roughly fifteen pieces, that I wove through waiting for the others to finish. Abstract art has never been my favorite – I can't help but think it's lines and colors I can reasonably copy even if I couldn't. There was one of layered circles that I loved the vibes of: bright, colorful, and fun.

Vikki joined me, also giving each piece a cursory look, but what truly captured our attention was an old olive-green steel door behind the last row of art. With its thick hinges, brass plate, and two sets of locks I knew it was the door to the vault without the help of the mural above it depicting its use in the 19th century.

I stared, surprised at how it was *right there* guarded only by a camera. Vikki kept daring me to get close, wanting me to take a photo of her pretending to open it, but I've always had a healthy respect, or perhaps fear, for authority. I couldn't bring myself to get closer than three feet and was hesitant to take her photo.

When Michele found us, she immediately pressed her ear against the door and placed her hand on the combination lock dial. "Take a picture!" she laughed while Vikki pulled out her phone. I nervously glanced around, on the lookout for security. Would we get thrown out? Arrested?

Seconds after the photo op finished, a bank staff member walked by. Michele boldly asked if the door led to the vault. It wasn't, we were assured, though it had led to the safety deposit boxes in the bank's history. The actual vault had more security, but leadership thought the old door looked cool and kept it. The only thing on the other side were offices. It made me feel foolish for my previous paranoia, but better than safe than sorry.

Maritime Museum

With cash in our pockets, we zipped up and headed toward the harbor. We'd taken the same route yesterday with the food tour, but now took the time to look at the boats and plaques along the way as we enjoyed better weather. The day felt colder, but we didn't have to worry about rain as we read about the history of Iceland's fishing industry and the harbor.

Reykjavik's harbor had been created by dredging, just streets away from main street shops and restaurants. Fishing might not be the industry powerhouse it used to be for the country, but there's still a fair number of fishing boats that call Reykjavik's harbor home. They bobbed in the water between cruise ships, coast guard vessels, and small whale sightseeing boats.

We walked the harbor's edge, and as always when I'm near water, I peered into the depths to look for fish. It was dark and murky, hiding any fish that might have been there, but we did see jellyfish. They were bright white and roughly the size of my palm, swimming just below the surface. Fish I like to see just to see, but jellyfish have always captured my attention like butterflies or finches. They're a flash of color compared to their background that moves slowly and gracefully in a way I can watch for hours. Sometimes, when I'm tired of songbirds on CatTV while working from home, I'll put on a video of jellyfish. Only for an hour though, my cat isn't interested in them nearly as much as she is birds.

We continued walking, and I found myself impressed by the lack of a fishy smell for a working harbor. Oh, you knew exactly where you were, but perhaps the cold or the harbor being used for more than fishing kept the scent to salt, damp wood, and in one spot, the scent of paint as we watched an industrial fishing boat get a touch-up. I'm not sure what surprised me more about that image – how short the boat was or what looked like very comfortable apartments with business on the first floor fifteen feet away. It was obvious that Reykjavik's waterfront was an integrated part of the city – work, home, and pleasure.

Passing ticket stands for boat tours, we approached a dock hosting a few museums including our target for the morning – the Reykjavik Maritime Museum.

An old wooden trawler sat out front, arranged on supports out of the water but close enough to smell the brine and fish. I grew up on the Detroit River, watching international shipping freighters, and so my idea of big boats is probably skewed. The plaques on the harbor walk made trawlers look short and squat, shorter than a ranch house, but as we got close to the trawler in front of the museum it was hard not to be impressed by its size. It towered above us, roughly 4x my height from the bottom of the hull to the top cabin, and certainly seemed capable of slowly coming into port with tons of fish.

"Take a picture!" Mom said, walking over wet rocks to approach the trawler and strike a pose at its base. I'm glad she's a communicator, my sister usually just stands somewhere, makes noises to get my attention, and then just poses.

"Let me set a timer," Vikki called back, already setting her phone on a cement step, before skipping down to join us.

No matter what angle we tried, we couldn't get us and the top of the boat in a single shot. These things sit *deep* in the water.

The Maritime Museum was small. It also had a very narrow scope, providing a deep dive into Iceland's fishing industry. There was only one exhibit that didn't, detailing the archaeological process around exploring and identifying the wreck of a 17th-century Dutch merchant ship called Melckmeyt. While not a part of the city's exhibit while I was there, there is a VR experience of diving down to see it that lives online.[1]

The permanent exhibits walked us through a range of information about Iceland's fishing history. We learned about the fish in the surrounding area, and I was fascinated that like tree rings, fish ear bones develop rings that you can use to determine their age. They're called otoliths.[2] There were also detailed looks at the advancement and specialization of fishing equipment. I ran my fingers over nets created with different types of nylon with tighter and tighter weaves.

---

1. Youtube. *Virtual Dive on the wreck of the Mlckmeyt (1659).* John McMarthy. 2020 https://www.youtube.com/watch?v=hovKu1bi7kA

2. Florida Fish and Wildlife Conservation Commission. *Introduction to Ageing Fish: What Are Otoliths?* 2023 https://myfwc.com/research/saltwater/fish/age-growth-lab/ageing-fish-otoliths/

Some holes I could stick an arm through, others, only a finger. There were recordings of witness testimonies of infamous sea wrecks. That far north, in water that cold, death was common for shipwrecked sailors. Human bodies just couldn't last long.

Tucked to the side of a chance to try on fisherman gear was a small display showing a clip of two large ships nearly colliding on the water. I found myself *very* invested when the voice-over indicated it was a Royal Navy ship doing its best to damage an Icelandic Coast Guard vessel. Why in the world would the UK do that?

The answer is the Cod Wars,[3] and I wish the museum had more than that single display about it. The video had a rubbernecking quality to it, but fishing rights seem like such a silly reason to go to war, especially three times from 1958 to 1976. And yet, the Cod Wars weren't just legal disputes and grumbling over who could fish where. There were attacks on ships and catch sabotages. The International Court of Justice and NATO were indirectly involved,[4] with Iceland making threats that would have impacted the Cold War.

It sounded so *huge* learning about it, I was shocked I never heard of it before. But I feel like that's a common complaint about any education – there are unexpected, shocking gaps. Like how my awareness of the AIDS crisis was pretty much nil until I watched the movie adaption of RENT and had questions. Or the history behind Juneteenth, which I'd only become aware of in the past five years. There

---

3. Wikipedia. *Cod Wars*. 2023 https://en.wikipedia.org/wiki/Cod_Wars

4. Atlas Obscura *How Iceland Beat the British in the Four Cod Wars*. Natasha Frost. 2018 https://www.atlasobscura.com/articles/what-were-cod-wars

will forever be things I'm shocked I didn't know before. I'll just have to learn them now.

It didn't take us long to go through the museum, walking out of the final exhibit into what could only be the child's area. There was a play ramp to the side, crafted jellyfish hanging from the ceiling, and several hanging chairs. We helped ourselves to the free coffee and sat on couches, ignoring the rain hitting the windows, talking about our careers and listening to Michele share news about her family. She's so proud of all three of her sons.

With the large windows looking out onto grey skies and covered in racing raindrops, we sunk into our seats. Now on day two of our vacation, we were starting to relax into the holiday, focusing on each other and not lingering over what we left behind. Reykjavik felt slow, unhurried, and its small footprint meant travel between places never took long.

We nursed hot drinks and passed around phones to share pet photos. What a contrast to my trip with my mom the previous fall, where she accepted phone calls while we hiked the Olympic National Forest. I didn't know what made this trip different – the larger time zone difference, the city, or a greater sense of knowing we *needed* to relax.

Mom and Michele, working in emergency medicine, were always under stress and COVID hadn't helped. Mom's department at the hospital had been understaffed for years, despite bucking national trends by expanding its number of pediatric beds. Hospitals make more money from adults, leading to a closing of pediatric units,[5] and it's hard to get structural support, even as children's departments get busier from a lack of alternative options. It didn't help that she, and Michele, are in their 60s doing swing shift work that includes late nights and overnights. Wacky sleep schedules, an inability to leave when your shift is done (you can't just *leave* a patient), and the stress of saving lives made both of them very, *very* eager to retire. When my mom finally does, her number one priority will be to rest and recover.

Vikki had been stressed too, a combination of management issues, racism, and sexism at a string of companies she'd worked at over the past two years. She'd started a new job earlier that month. In fact, she had 24 hours between arriving in Chicago after an onsite training on the West Coast and taking off for Iceland - and had similarly been looking forward to the trip and a chance to disconnect.

I might have been the least stressed at the time, but I've had my issues. In hindsight, I'm pretty sure I hit burnout Nov 2021. It all became too much one day. I dropped everything nonessential - including ghosting the woman I'd been dating. I slowly eased into my volunteering leadership roles after a week of veg time, pushed on by the fact that we were in the middle of our biggest event of the year, but unless something absolutely required my presence I wasn't there. I spent weekends and weeknights mindlessly binging Teen Wolf. I didn't have the energy for anything else.

---

5. The New York Times. *As Hospitals Close Children's Units, Where Does that Leave Lachlan?* Emily Baumgaertner Oct 2022 https://www.nytimes.com/2022/10/11/health/pediatric-closures-hospitals.html

Thankfully, my manager could tell I was stretched thin, and we slowly worked on reducing my workload. I didn't start to recover until April 2022 when my hours dropped to 45 a week, but my motivation and capacity to write stories didn't return until mid-July. That return of creativity made me realize how long I hadn't had it, almost a year, which in turn made me face just how long I'd been overwhelmed. Now, almost a year after I hit my breakpoint, I'm fiercely protective of my work-life balance and take time for self-care. Long-term stress is serious, and I knew an Icelandic vacation wasn't going to fix it for anyone. But it was a reprieve we were all dedicated to feeling.

Blue Lagoon

"Lunch?" Vikki asked once the rain tapered off. "Can we go back to the fish soup place from yesterday?"

We made our way back to Street Food but not before stopping at the liquor store. The grocery store hadn't carried any alcohol. Over concern about not finding any wine during our five-night, six-day tour around the island, and knowing we'd want to relax after long days, we had to stock up. Michele scanned bottles with an app while Mom dithered over a small bottle of Baileys, but ultimately, we slipped four bottles of wine into a bag before heading to lunch.

The bright yellow décor of Street Food caught our attention yesterday, and now it served as an identifier out of a string of fish and chips offerings. I forewent the fish soup, though Vikki excitedly ordered a big bowl. I tried the lobster soup and was amazed by how hot it was. In America, I feel soup is served at a temperature ready to eat but I had to blow on my spoon for every single mouthful. This became a minor issue as we looked at our watches and realized the scheduled pick-up for our evening activity was rapidly approaching.

We started shoveling food into our mouths, escaping with minimal tastebud injuries.

The march back to the hotel was a frantic, head-down affair in the rain that we were quickly becoming adept at. After hastily packing our backpacks, we booked it to the bus stop. We made it with eight minutes to spare.

We chatted with the minibus driver, who explained how he fell into the career. He used to be a teacher at the local college, but when Iceland declared bankruptcy in 2008 he lost his job. Like the Cod Wars, I found this bit of Icelandic history fascinating, this time because I hadn't realized a country *could* declare bankruptcy. As it turns out, it's not that uncommon. The US itself has done it, but Iceland holds the record as the biggest systematic banking collapse in history.[1] The country has mostly recovered, but you can still see the marks. Our driver's college never reopened.

We pulled into a location called "Bus Hostel", which while a cute name heralded the annoying task of switching buses. We joined other travelers on a much larger bus to our destination – the Blue Lagoon.

I'd been before during my first trip to Iceland and found it delightful. Michele's fondness for spas made Blue Lagoon a must on this trip too. I'll admit it's touristy, but the basic package is worth it. I'd forgo the extras.

Blue Lagoon is roughly an hour out of Reykjavik, surrounded by an 800-year-old lava field. The landscape we drove through was

---

1. The Business Standard. *6 Major Countries That Went Bankrupt In Recent Times.* 2022 https://www.tbsnews.net/world/6-major-countries-went-bankrupt-recent-times-453426

lumpy piles of stone, covered in vibrant green moss. I've never seen anything like it in the world, but the view couldn't capture me enough to prevent a nap. I hadn't quite adjusted to the six-hour time difference yet.

We stepped off the bus to harsh wind, then walked through lava piles ten feet tall to the spa entrance. Mom encouraged us to explore before swimming, so we followed a small walking path through the lava field, taking in the truly alien landscape. The white silica made the water reflect a robin's egg blue, a striking color against black lava stone.[2] Steam rising from the water added to the foreign feeling, as if at any moment it could reveal something unexpected.

We dipped our hands in the water, hoping for something warm to guard against the wind, but it was lukewarm at best. In all our photos, my hands are shoved deep into my coat pockets to protect my fingers.

Walking into the spa complex was impressive, it'd certainly been built with tourists in mind. Compared to the tight spaces we'd seen in Reykjavik, the locker rooms were wide and tiled with grey porcelain. We went through quickly, making our way to the spa. The water was the same robin's egg blue we'd seen outside, lapping against black lava rock on the pool's edge. The pool itself was deep and sprawling with a variety of small offshoots. Wooden pedestrian bridges connected paths through the rocks.

I slipped into the water and headed toward a small cave with two wide mouths, lined with submerged ledges. I took a seat and breathed

---

2. Inspired by Iceland. *Why Is The Blue Lagoon Blue?* 2023 https://www.inspiredbyiceland.com/travel/why-is-the-blue-lagoon-blue/

in steam, catching not even a hint of sulfur or chlorine. Vikki joined me, sinking to her shoulders. "This is nice."

"Come on!" Mom said after a moment. "Let go explore."

"And find the bar," Michele added. "Tickets came with a drink!"

Leaving the cave, the cool, almost cold air made me shiver as I walked through the spa. The water came up to the bottom of my rib cage, so I walked in a crouch to stay warm. The steam was thick enough to hide the far side of the spa, but around the bar was a crowd of people with drinks in hand we could clearly see. We ordered, eager to try local brands, and ended up chatting with a couple from Houston, Texas. One drink quickly turned to more.

The slow, relaxed mood from the museum seeped deeper into our bones, helped by alcohol and warm water. Well plied, I find Somersby cider sweet and crisp and delicious, we headed across the main pool. The water level rose significantly, almost up to my shoulders, which meant it had to have been a little deeper than five feet. I found myself pulling Vikki along with one hand, the other holding my half-finished cider above the water. At 5 ft 1 in, she couldn't be bothered to swim and needed the support.

While the Blue Lagoon had been labeled one of the 25 natural wonders of the world in 2012 by National Geographic,[3] the spa is man-made. The designation came from the unique properties of the water, a geothermally heated mix of ocean water, freshwater, and several minerals. The most prominent of them is silica, which

---

3. Blue Lagoon. *Is the Blue Lagoon a Wonder of the World?* 2019 https://www.bluelagoon.com/stories/is-the-blue-lagoon-a-wonder-of-the-world

is reported to have anti-aging properties and is known to improve psoriasis and eczema,[4] but there are other minerals in the water too.

On the other side of the main pool, we held out our hands to staff at the mud hunt. They ladled runny, white mud into our cupped palms. This was our silica mask. It went on like a clay mask, thick but spreadable, and we were told to keep it on for thirty minutes. Grabbing the drinks, we found a free ledge in a nearby cove and sat in the water.

As we waited for the masks to dry, Vikki let slip she'd never learned to swim. This appalled the moms of the group. Michele had learned to swim from a young age, as had my mother. My swimming lessons started at nine months and accelerated once my family moved to downriver Detroit. Living close to water meant swimming was a survival skill, not just a summer activity.

Determined to help Vikki out, Michele did her best to teach Vikki how to float, but it was a lost cause. Despite the water only reaching Vikki's armpits in the cove, she couldn't relax enough to float and frequently tensed up. Her three glasses of wine didn't help. They made her more conscious about compensating for any misjudgment and more paranoid about water around her face.

Poor swimming lesson aside, we enjoyed the spa. Walking from cove to cove, doing yoga in shallow spots, soaking up the warmth. We spent nearly three hours in the water. The webbing between my fingers was wrinkly by the time we left.

---

4. Blue Lagoon. *Academic papers.* 2023 https://www.bluelagoon.com/academic-papers

We'd planned on a quick dinner, swinging by a fast-food place as we walked back to the hotel, but fast food in Iceland is rare. I didn't see a single American chain in the city. No Starbucks, Panera, Subway, or Burger King. There were rumors of a KFC between downtown and the airport, but none of us wanted that.

Iceland isn't the only country I've been to lacking American brands – Ethiopia's government also curbed the opening of international franchises to foster the growth of local businesses – and that meant we could only guess at how quickly our to-go order would be.

We ordered from a gyro shop we spied on our walk to the hotel. While Mom and Michele waited for the order, Vikki and I headed to a sweet shop down the street. They only sold loukomathi, the Greek version of donut holes, and thus the perfect dessert for the night. One of the servers was delighted at my pronunciation but was crestfallen when I admitted that while I'm ethnically Greek, my knowledge of the language is scarce. I think he slipped us an extra anyway, and Vikki gave me a nudge and head tilt toward the guy.

Rolling my eyes at her, I stuck a honey-covered loukomathi in my mouth as we met up with Mom and Michele. At the hotel, we hung up our swimsuits and I hoped they dried before we left the next morning – we had to be at the bus stop by 7:30 am. The early departure didn't stop us from opening a bottle of wine and chatting the rest of the evening about what we were excited to see. Michele was already looking forward to our second spa, while Mom was eager for the glacier hike and Vikki wanted to see *everything*. The aurora, however, was on everyone's mind.

"I hope we see it every night," Vikki sighed as we slipped into bed.

Day 3

Ring Tour Start!

We woke bright and early, forgoing a morning stretch to pack our bags. My swimsuit, despite attempts to wash it out the previous night, was crunchy. Still, it was dry and became wrapping for a wine bottle.

We rolled out of the hotel between dawn and full light, the streets empty and the sky grey but lit. Our suitcase wheels clacked against cobblestones and asphalt cracks as we went along, hoping to find a coffee shop open. Sadly, we found none.

The bus stop was an unnamed green space, featuring a hill upon which stood a statue of the Norwegian Ingolfur Arnarson, whose family in 874 became the first permanent settlers of Iceland. He stands in Viking gear next to the mast of a ship, looking down at one of the few busy streets that cut through Reykjavík. Due to the nature of our bus instructions (pick up at 8 am, but due to variances from picking up at other stops it could arrive between 7:30 am and 8:30 am) we had a lot of time to kill. I walked around Ingolfur's pedestal, climbing the steps up the hill to circle the base before heading down to the park's edges. Between the cold and my flat feet, standing was uncomfortable so I made many loops as we traded off who watched our suitcases.

Around eight, Mom and Michele left to see if any of the local coffee shops opened. They came back empty-handed. I nestled further into my coat, zipped to my chin, and found myself distracted by the increasing number of tourists gathering. Almost every tour company used this bus stop, and many had multiple tours leaving a day. Determining which bus was ours became a game that we lost many, many times.

What eventually picked us up was a grey minibus with the tour company's name, Arctic Adventures, on its hood. It pulled a trailer for our suitcases, and the driver-cum-tour guide who hopped off to take our bags was awake and chipper. With blonde scruff and an Icelandic accent, he introduced himself and took our bags.

"Grab a seat," he said, pointing at the bus's open doors. "I'll have these loaded in a minute, and then we have more people to pick up."

The bus was a Benz with black and copper pleather seats that offered USB ports, small holding areas, and footrests. Way roomier than an airplane, with free wifi to boot. Most of the seats had been taken already; our tour had booked the full eighteen the bus could fit. Like us, the other passengers looked eager but not quite awake. I suspected no one had found coffee.

We didn't need caffeine once we left the city, the excitement waking us all up. We didn't want to miss a thing.

The Golden Circle

Day one of the tour was, to put it bluntly, the most touristy day. We did the Golden Circle, a trio of natural sites that were not that far from Reykjavik and so are the basis of many, many day tours. I'd done it on my previous trip, but I was eager to see them again. Moreover, I was eager to share them.

I'd loved my previous trip, a week seeing incredible things amongst a topography that at times reminded me of New Zealand, which often led to mental connections between Lord of the Rings and other fantastic worlds and stories. I'd loved it enough that I'd come back for a second, more thorough trip, and I wanted my travel buddies to have the same experience. To fall in love with a beautiful country and stare at its majesty.

I don't know if it's how the roads are built, but both times I've done the Golden Circle I've done it in the same order. We started with Þingvellir National Park, which has been recognized as a UNESCO World Heritage Site for its geological and historical significance.

In 930, the Alþing general assembly was established and continued to meet near the river Öxará until 1789.[1] For two weeks a year, the assembly set laws and settled disputes. Fragments of turf and stone booths from the meeting area are visible today in Þingvellir.

The Alþing's founding started the Icelandic Commonwealth, but after the country declared fealty to the Kingdom of Norway in 1262, the Alþing's focus shifted away from executive power into legislative and judicial roles. Eventually, the Alþing's power faded, shed to ruling kings, but it was brought back in 1844 by the King of Denmark. It currently meets and is considered the world's longest-running parliament.[2]

I could detect a bit of pride in our guide's tone as he talked about it, the park and its history are important to the locals, but what brings most tourists is the geographical features of the park. We were given roughly 90 minutes to explore them, which felt both enough and not enough time.

First up was a small hike to Öxarárfoss, or 'ox-tail waterfall'. We walked up a staircase to a scattering of basalt boulders, and there it was, falling down a small cliff onto rocks and throwing up a slight spray. Michele pulled out her camera, a DSL I hadn't realized she brought. She found her spot and snapped a photo. I wasn't nearly as picky, pulling out my phone to snap a photo from the end of a wooden platform.

---

1. Thingvellir National Park. *Heart of Iceland.* 2023 https://www.thingvellir.is/en/

2. Adventures *Thingvellier National Park | Complete Guide.* 2023 https://adventures.com/iceland/attractions/national-parks/thingvellir/

Once upon a time, I'd had a hand-held point-and-shoot camera, but with the way technology advanced, my Pixel was enough for me. Plus, on time that handheld camera slipped out of my backpack when I jumped a rock, leaving the lens edge dented. It still worked (and still might if I charged it), but I'd rather not have to worry about an additional piece of technology nowadays. Phones are fine for the casual photographer.

I didn't know it at the time, but Öxarárfoss was the first stop of the trip that had served as a Game of Thrones shooting location. Many shots of Westeros were created on the island, and Öxarárfoss served as the Bloody Gate that marks the entrance of the Eyrie.

We left the waterfall behind to continue along the Öxará river, almost black that cloudy day, until the path turned and sloped up. Now we walked between cliff sides, noting warnings of rockfalls and stopping to read a particular alarming display about how not that long ago a giant hole had shown up in the path and the bridge we stood on spanned it. And then, there it was, the view that draws thousands of tourists a day.

The continental divide.

Continental divides are where continental plates meet, forming impressive geographical features. The United States has several, but most people refer to them as the Rocky Mountains or the San Andreas Fault. The Rocky Mountains were formed by a combination of volcanic eruptions, but also the Farallon plate sliding under the North American plate, wrinkling the earth.[3] It's not an active divide,

---

3. Wikipedia. *Rocky Mountains. Geology.* 2023 https://en.wikipedia.org/wiki/Rocky_Mountains#Geology

unlike the San Andreas Fault. There, the Pacific and North American plates are sliding against each other to cause the earthquakes California is known for. [4] It's a blessing I hadn't experienced one the year I lived in San Francisco.

Neither of those situations is happening in Iceland. No, what we looked out over was the impact of the Eurasian and North American plates drifting *away* from each other to create a rift valley. They've been moving apart roughly an inch a year, [5] and in that space is marshland and an ever-growing lake called Þingvallavatn. The lake has a rich, unique ecosystem as it was glacier-formed and cut off from the ocean.

At the rim of the lake is the Silfra Fissure, home of the clearest freshwater in the world where visibility can extend 330 ft. The reason for this is the fresh glacier water that fills it, creating a gentle current that prevents bacteria from growing and muddying the water. Perhaps during my next trip, I'll snorkel or dive in the fissure.

I wish we could have taken in the view for longer, but my phone screen was riddled with raindrops after taking only three photos and thick cloud cover meant I could barely see the other side of the rift. We scurried into the local gift shop, finally able to snag coffee and breakfast. We didn't have enough time to fully enjoy it before we had to be back on the bus. It was obvious our group was the last to arrive,

---

4. Wikipedia. *San Andreas Fault.* 2023 https://en.wikipedia.org/wiki/San_Andreas_Fault

5. Adventures *Thingvellier National Park | Complete Guide.* 2023 https://adventures.com/iceland/attractions/national-parks/thingvellir/

but I also hadn't felt like we'd lingered anywhere. Still, I felt bad for being late.

I vowed to be more diligent at our next stop, the Geysir Geothermal Park.

I'd been confused at first, didn't the location have a name other than geyser area?, but it turns out the word 'geyser' was derived from the name of the park, [6] which holds the first documented geysers in Europe. [7] The name of the large active geyser there is Strokkur, and it regularly erupts every seven minutes. We sat on a nearby bench, munching sandwiches from the gift shop, as we watched several cycles of hot water launch 100 ft into the air.

We walked the rest of the park, glad the rain had stopped but wary of the mud. None of us had worn sturdy hiking shoes, just gym shoes and day hikers. When younger, I'd sprained my ankles almost every year after a bad soccer season, and loose tendons and weak ankles mean I still regularly do *something* to injure them. I've not had a sprain bad enough to require crutches or piggybacks since 2009, but I'd hoped not to bring out my ankle braces on day three. Michele and Mom placed their feet gingerly too – they both have knee problems, and Michele had been wearing her knee brace all day.

None of the geysers in the park were very large, or smelly, but I found myself entranced by the colors in the pools of heated water. I'm sure there were silica deposits, even if the blue didn't match the

---

6. Arctic Adventures. *6 Days Around Iceland Adventure.* 2023 https://adventures.is/iceland/multiday-tours/6-day-tour-around-iceland-adventure/

7. Reykjavik Excursions. *Your Ultimate Guide to the Golden Circle in Iceland.* 2022https://www.re.is/blog/your-ultimate-guide-to-the-golden-circle-in-iceland/

Blue Lagoon. The Lagoon is more of a robin's egg blue, and this was a turquoise that recalled images of Caribbean beach screen savers. I was tempted to touch the water, but each pool was roped off. I did manage to dip my fingers in the runoff from a few, and it wasn't hot at all. That said, to quote Vikki, I like to cook myself in the shower. I frequently shower in water between 87 and 92F, and it makes Vikki wail because, apparently, cold showers are better for your pores.

Despite our best attempts to watch the time, we ended up being last on the bus again. I don't know if our fellow travelers were faster walkers, more paranoid about the time, or tired of the sights quicker than us, but I resigned myself to the knowledge that our group would be the slow pokes. There were worse things to be.

The third stop on the Golden Circle was Gullfoss, another waterfall, but a million times more impressive than the one we'd seen at Þingvellir National Park.

By the time we stepped off the bus, the rain had cleared. I took a moment to bask in a sunbeam before scampering after Michele and Mom. They expressed a hearty desire to not be the last ones this stop. I think they felt self-conscious of their age and how it slowed them down; half the bus was 25 to 35.

Mom always has a high awareness of her image. Sometimes it works in her favor because she has an eye for clothes and hair, but other times I can see the harm from her perceived image being different than what she wants. Mom prides herself on her looks, she has several stories about stopping cars when younger, and Dad admits that her hip swing is what caught his attention. Getting older, getting more stressed due to work, and having less time for self-care the more she needs it, has hit her hard. Being late to the bus turned into another example of her age and lack of fitness.

Part of the reason we might have frequently been late was picture taking. Michele's large camera took incredible photos but required time to uncap the lens, make adjustments, and so on. Vikki also developed a fascination with the local plants, crouching low to take photos of flowers or stems of grass stalks heavy with seed. While part of my lack of photo-snapping was knowing we would share and having photos from my previous trip when the weather had been sunnier, I also wanted to avoid the overabundance of digital photos.

My first camera had SD cards. I had two that together made up almost a gig of space (paltry compared to now but a lot at the time) and I'd fill them with shots of anything that captured my attention. Day to day I had no problem, 1G was several hundred photos, but I would run out of space on longer trips. I'd have to flip between three photos of a waterfall, delete two, and determine if a particular tree was interesting enough to be immortalized in a digital file. If I didn't, there'd be no space on the camera for photos on the last day.

The last time I used that camera was in the Peace Corps, taking over two years of photos that I kept having to transfer to my laptop. The folder grew, developing subfolders, including one for each summer camp I helped run. For one camp, we made a slide show to play for the girls who attended. A fellow volunteer commented that video was all she needed to save from the week-long event. In two years, she might not remember the names of all fifty campers. Would lose the memories and context behind each shot. Maybe 10, 20% of the photos would resonate with her in the future.

My dad said something similar when I was younger, scrolling through images he'd uploaded to the family desktop. "With digital cameras, it's so easy to take a photo so you take a gazillion. Do you really need all of them?"

In short, no. I didn't need twenty photos of the same thing from slightly different angles with slightly different camera settings. So as I skipped down the steps to the waterfall, I tracked the path. What three spots were the views I wanted to take a photo of? I took the lead, hoping to subconsciously nudge my travel partners to limit their photo lingering to keep up. I was moderately successful.

Gullfoss translates to 'golden waterfall'. It consists of two tiers of falls; a shorter one on top, and then a larger drop before the river snakes through a gorge it's cut. Water falls in total 105 ft and during the summer when the water flow is heaviest, just under 5,000 cubic feet of water tumbles to the bottom every second. [8]

The amount and breath of the water falling makes Gullfoss a rainbow magnet, even on a day recovering from grayness. Michele pointed out a faint rainbow while we stood on slick rocks next to the top of the second tier, mist droplets collecting on our clothes.

Gullfoss is one of my favorite waterfalls in Iceland. It's breathtaking, stunning from any angle. It's also incredible that, unlike other powerful waterfalls, it hasn't been turned into a hydroelectric dam. There'd been an attempt in the early 20th century when the man who owned the land loaned it out with a lease that gave renters the right to do what they wanted. He regretted it once plans for the dam were

---

8. Wikipedia. *Gulfoss*. 2022 https://en.wikipedia.org/wiki/Gullfoss

presented, but it was his daughter, Sigridur Tomasdottir, who made the difference. [9]

Like many activists, she caused scenes. She threatened to throw herself from the falls. She walked the (then) unpaved 134 miles of road between Gullfoss and Reykjavik multiple times. She built awareness of what was happening at a national scale, which Icelanders weren't too pleased about. They're a very green-minded country.

The contract was annulled, and the lawyer instrumental in the case, Sveinn Bjornsson, became Iceland's first president. So when I say that Icelanders are very green-minded, I truly mean that. Preservation and dedication to nature has been a priority of its leaders for years. The result, a stunningly beautiful country, speaks for itself.

There's a plaque to Sigridur at the bottom of the stairs that leads to the Gullfoss viewing trail, praising her for not only bringing awareness to the need to preserve nature but also for not being tempted by foreign investments. Which, in hindsight, might also have impacted the lack of Starbucks in Iceland.

The country still likes foreign money; it relies on tourism and there has been a lot of development to encourage cash flow. Next to Gullfoss was a large parking lot, as well as a moderately sized gift shop. Mom huffed, sad we didn't have the time to shop. I would have been okay with more time at all these locations too, not to shop but to not feel as rushed, but Mom has always been a 'thing' person. I only

---

9. Guide to Iceland. *The Ultimate Guide to Iceland's Golden Circle*. Richard Chapman. 2023 (https://guidetoiceland.is/best-of-iceland/top-9-detours-on-the-golden-circle

needed two souvenirs from the trip: photos and an item that would represent *something*.

We weren't the last to the bus this time, and our tour guide calmed us down by saying he didn't care if we were a few minutes late, eyeing the brace Michele had been wearing all day. Besides, he said, he'd never seen these stops so busy. He blamed that day's arrival of several cruise ships, unloading thousands of people of which a fair number had most likely taken a Golden Circle tour.

He predicted the crowds would thin out soon, we'd be hitting spots a bit late for day trips that needed to return to the city. Plus, day two of our tour was the last day of events feasible to do as day trips from Reykjavik. We looked forward to it.

South Coast Falls

Most of Iceland's famous waterfalls are on the south coast. As we left the greater Reykjavik area, finally driving on the Icelandic ring road, we made pitstops to see several of them.

The first was Seljalandsfoss. It doesn't have the weight and power of Gullfoss, producing no roar from a fall so wispy wind can blow it away before it reaches the bottom. It is, however, almost double the height[1] and is known for the shallow cave behind the waterfall.

When we arrived, we still had sunlight and clear skies, but the wind picked up. It tugged at my pants and blew spray into the air. There was a small outcropping before the waterfall we lined up to take photos at, and my favorites are of Michele's scarf slapping her in the face.

Due to the weather, the hike to the cave behind the waterfall was super wet. I pulled my hands out of my pockets, placing them on

---

1. Wikipedia. *Seljalandsfoss*. 2023 https://en.wikipedia.org/wiki/Seljalandsfoss

rocks for balance for a series of small scrambles, and we took our time finding our footing.

"I wish I wore my boots," Michele said as she joined me on a small outlook, peering down into the pool of water Seljalandsfoss emptied into.

"Same," I answered.

Arctic Adventures had called all the hikes easy or moderate, which was true, but that doesn't always mean flat, even trails.

"You're knee okay?"

"I'm good, Gin. Nothing ibuprofen won't fix later."

"Sorry."

"What for?"

I truth, I felt bad for misremembering the hikes. This was my second trip to Seljalandsfoss. I should have recalled the slanted rocks and gravel in the cave and recommended that we wear our hiking boots instead of sticking them in our suitcases for the day. Any ungroomed trail, no matter how easy, could hold an ankle trap, and this small loop was full of them.

"These shoes are fine," Michele said. "I'm sure today isn't the only day we wish we'd done something different. Now come on, your Mom's almost at the bottom. Let's catch up."

We moved on to Skógafoss, or forest waterfall, which while falling from the same height as Seljalandsfoss is much more powerful. It's got breath at 82ft wide and falls into a pool of water that laps at a flat stone beach. While Gullfoss is viewed from above, and Seljalandsfoss falls into a pool inside a small divot you walk around, a bold adventurer could put on waders and stand under Skógafoss if they wanted.

Of course, I'm sure it would be hard to withstand the shit-ton of water pressure.

We walked down the stone beach, rocks clunking under our feet, until the spray made it hard to see each other. We huddled together and stuck our tongues out to catch the spray-like rain. The spray collected into a large cloud that slowly rolled down the river, which looked deceptively small considering the amount of water falling.

This was one of the few waterfalls with a myth. A man named Þrasi is said to have hidden a chest of gold behind the falls, with one end visible through the water. Three local men tried to pull it free by hooking the iron ring and pulling. But the chest was so heavy the only thing that happened was that the iron ring popped off. It was used as a church doorknocker for years before being placed in a local museum, but of the chest itself, there's been no sign.

We squinted, trying to see through the mist and water, but couldn't even see the rock behind the froth.

Vikki and I turned our attention to the stairs next to the waterfall. There were 450 of them, and we went up quickly, leaving Michele and Mom behind.

We passed sheep on the hillside, grazing on green grass, and on top of the cliff we found the river in a rougher state than below, full of small rapids as it ran through fields that reminded me of steppes. Vikki let out a sigh, taking in the view. Stretching around us was green, green, green, broken only by a small river delta and the tiny gravel parking lot.

"It's like Mongolia," Vikki said, turning in a circle. She hadn't been in roughly five years, and while she'd talked about the country somewhat, I'd never heard this type of longing from her before. She kept waxing about the view in a way that made me wonder if she was homesick for a place she'd only visited, clinging to the grazing sheep on the hillsides as she recalled her grandparents' flock.

As we made our eventual way down the stairs, Vikki insisted on a photo of her as close to the sheep as possible. Sadly, it wasn't close enough to satisfy her, which kicked off Vikki's number one goal of the trip – take a selfie with a sheep.

We had one last stop of the day – a black sand beach called Reynisfjara. Our guide called it a Game of Thrones filming location, which made Vikki excited. While I'd stopped watching the show at season five, she knew the scene our guide referenced and was buzzing.

Like most of the day, we arrived to dark, grey clouds and the area gave off somber, monochrome vibes between the sky, ocean, and sand. The beach's claim to fame is its basalt rock formations.[2] Crystallized pillars of black hexagons had been bundled together to form the mountains, and now water erosion showed them at various heights along the shore and in the interior of caves. They were formed by cooling lava, just like the beach sand, when the volcano Katla erupted centuries ago.

Reynisfjara is a look, don't touch beach. By which I mean, don't swim there. There are warnings about how quickly the tide changes, sneaker waves, and strong currents.[3] What our guide pressed us to

---

2. Reykjavik Excursions. *Reynisfjara Black Sand Beach in Iceland – Your Guide.* 2022 https://www.re.is/blog/reynisfjara-black-sand-beach-in-iceland/

3. Visit Iceland. *Warnings: Reynisfjara Beach Has Claimed The Lives of Visitors. Here Is How To Stay Safe.* 2023 https://www.visiticeland.com/article/reynisfjara-black-sand-beach-is-dangerous

remember was the temperature of the water. It was cold enough that your body would shut down in 10 minutes, faster than any rescue attempt could get to you.

Back on the bus, I was relieved to sit. We'd done a lot of walking. I did my best to stretch out my legs under the seat, watching the coast until it was too dark to see. We pulled up to our hotel, Adventure Hotel, after dark and almost an hour later than we'd expected.

It was in the middle of nowhere, as we'd been warned. A random building off a minor road at the bottom of a small cliff. This describes many of Iceland's hotels along the ring road. Reykjavik is the country's largest city with a population of 120,000, but the next largest is only 32,000. Of the towns we passed through on the tour, the average was under two thousand. Iceland's population is sparse and scattered; hotels run by local landlords are similarly distributed.

Our guide passed out room keys; Vikki and I shared while Mom and Michele had their own. We quickly scrambled to shower, dry, and dress. Our late arrival meant the hotel restaurant extended its kitchen hours for us, and I didn't want to keep the staff there later than needed.

The entire bus shared a table. While we'd spent the day in each other's company, there hadn't been much socialization. The bus had been quiet, listening to our tour guide or audio on our phones while we watched the landscape. During the hikes, everyone focused on seeing the waterfalls, squeezing in time for the bathroom, or taking in other views. Now, we got to meet our tourmates.

There was a surprising number of Australians, older couples and young solo travelers, taking advantage of Australia recently lifting COVID travel restrictions. There were two older American couples, plus two solo Asian-American women. A pair of cousins from America. No one was surprised to know we traveled as a set of four, but we did have to insist Vikki wasn't Michele's daughter. This wasn't a mother-daughter trip, for all that my mom likes to adopt my friends. Still, it made me happy that we got along well enough that people made the assumption.

Despite the bottles of wine squirreled away, we didn't open any that night. We felt exhausted and were eager to climb into bed after dinner. Vikki and I put out our clothing on the bathroom and room heaters: jackets, hats, gloves, socks. Between the rain and waterfall spray, our gear had gotten pretty wet.

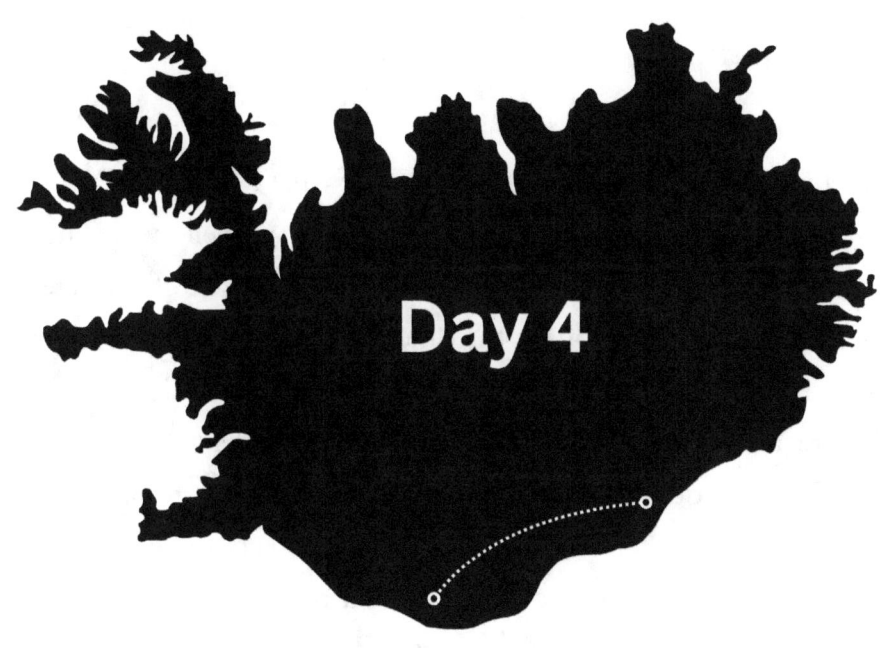

Feather River Canyon

Icelandic breakfast buffets reminded me of what I've seen in Europe – a variety of breads, butter and jam spreads, and deli meat. There was usually a small pastry of some kind and of course coffee and tea.

While we got to the bus at the time we'd been told, others in our group showed up first. We got the leftover seats – the entire back row.

I wasn't thrilled. I tend to get carsick in the back of vehicles, headachy and queasy in a way that makes me desperate for a cracked window to feel a breeze on my face. It comes and goes, and I'm more sensitive in the back seat of low cars that make frequent turns or lane switches. The window I sat next to didn't open. Worse, the last row was elevated to the point that my eyeline was above the window. I leaned my head on the side of the car and forced myself to nap, thankful the road was flat, the curves wide, and the traffic limited.

The bus pulled up to a gorge called Fjaðrárgljúfur which wasn't on the itinerary Arctic Adventures provided. When we looked to our guide he shrugged, saying we had the time and he thought it was a fantastic place to visit. He was absolutely right – it was one of my favorite spots on the trip and everyone who posted a photo had friends and family leaving comments with hearts and questions about it, wanting to add to their future itineraries.

For all that it wasn't officially on the tour, Fjaðrárgljúfur isn't unknown. Some drive-yourself tours recommend it as a stop, and it was featured in the music video for Justin Bieber's "I'll Show You". [1] A video none of us on the bus had seen, but it made the canyon such a popular attraction access had been blocked for a time for preservation efforts.[2] It's recovered at this point, with ropes preventing tourists from walking the exact path Bieber did. Probably for the best – that spit of a trail was on a narrow rock ledge where a foot slip could send you on a 300ft fall.

The hike started with us going up a hill, then transitioned to a walk along the top of the canyon. Compared to yesterday's hikes, the trail was wide and well-maintained with parts covered in terraced rubber for traction on rainy days. The A-to-B hike was roughly three miles round trip with the river snaking along 330 ft below. While there's a lot of basalt in Iceland, the walls of the canyon were palagonite, a white-grey rock that was covered in moss to the point where it all looked soft.

The canyon itself captured me, but above it was the green steppe landscape that caught Vikki's attention the previous day. In the

---

1. Arctic Adventures. *Fjadrargljufur.* 2023 https://adventures.is/iceland/attractions/fjadrargljufur/

2. Laidback Trip. *A Travel Guide to Fjadrargljufur Canyon.* Lucie Hermankova and Martin Tychtl. 2023 https://www.laidbacktrip.com/posts/fjadrargljufur-canyon-guide

morning light, the grass was inviting and we saw sheep on the cliff edges. They were nimble as goats, but they reminded me of corgis. They have round, pert rears with wool that's stringier than sheep I've seen in America. They're also short and stocky like corgis; tiny legs and low centers of gravity.

Fjaðrárgljúfur ends, or starts I suppose, where two different waterfalls meet: Mögárfoss and Fjaðrárfoss. Fjaðrárfoss flows right under the viewing platform, which is aimed at the slightly larger Mögárfoss.[3] Against the dark, wet rock, the water is a stark white streak zigzagging down the rocks.

As the day was bright and sunny, everyone on the bus lingered on the trail back to get their dose of vitamin D. We picked up from dinner last night, getting to know other travelers as we walked in small groups that merged and split and merged. I talked to Nathan, a Navy pilot who had made Iceland one of many stops for his current vacation, as well as a few of the Australian women. I'm not sure how much Vikki and Michele talked to our tourmates, they trailed behind going from photo spot to photo spot. Mom, on the other hand, was in her element. She loves talking to people and laughed with someone or another going up and down the trail. I smiled watching her chat with the group of Australian women, easily half her age, and fitting in seamlessly.

I'm so glad the bus got along – it would have been a very uncomfortable tour if we hadn't!

---

3. Guide to Iceland. *The Picturesque Fjaðrárgljúfur Canyon in South-Iceland*. Regína Hrönn Ragnarsdóttir. 2023 https://guidetoiceland.is/connect-with-locals/regina/the-picturesque-fjadrargljufur-canyon-in-south-iceland

The easy hike was a great start to the morning, something that made the whole bus happy and rosy-cheeked. It was also a stark contrast to the next item on the itinerary – a glacier hike.

Falling Glacier

Glaciers had been Mom's request number one request. "I wanna do what you did, Ginny," she told me on more than one phone call or email chain.

I've done a few things on glaciers: a hike on the Franz Jose Glacier in New Zealand and an experience called Into The Glacier on my previous trip to Iceland that involved walking through a man-made cave at the top of the Langjökull Glacier. For this trip we couldn't do both – go in and on a glacier – but any tour that didn't include something got knocked off the list. Artic Adventures' tour included a glacier activity regardless of the time of year, which was the primary reason we'd gone with them.

We pulled into Vatnajökull National Park, which is, quite frankly, huge. Established in 2008 and named after the glacier Vatnajökull (translating to water glacier), the park encompasses that very glacier and the extensive surrounding area.

The glacier itself is the second largest ice cap in Europe, and the largest in Iceland, at 3,000 square miles with an average ice thickness of 1,250 ft.[1] From Vatnajökull form 30 different outlet glaciers, tongues or fingers of ice that flow down mountains and valleys from the ice's peak. The entire park is 8,800 square miles, roughly 14% of Iceland.[2] It's Europe's second-largest national park, surpassed only by Yugyd Va in Russia. In 2019, the park became a UNESCO World Heritage Site.[3]

Iceland is known as the Land of Fire and Ice and the Vatnajökull region is a prime example of why. There's a complex interaction between glaciers and eruptions and the geothermal heat from Iceland's active tectonic rift. Within the park are ten volcanoes, eight of which are under glaciers, and two of them are Iceland's most active.

Road No 1, the ring road we followed, weaves in and out of Vatnajökull National Park. The road hadn't been finished until 1974 with the completion of a bridge over the river Skeiðará. While we drove over the bridge that morning, the river changed course in 2009 leaving very little evidence of an obstacle that had been such a travel bane.[4] This type of geographical shifting in the area is common with the largest caused by jökulhlaup, sudden floods of glacier water following a volcanic eruption. The last one in 1996 had been pow-

---

1. Global Alliance of National Parks. *Vatnajokull National Park*. 2023 https://national-parks.org/iceland/vatnajokull

2. Wikipedia. *Vatnajökull National Park*. 2023 https://en.wikipedia.org/wiki/Vatnaj%C3%B6kull_National_Park

3. UNESCO World Heritage Convention. *Vatnajökull National Park - Dynamic Nature of Fire and Ice*. 2023 https://whc.unesco.org/en/list/1604

4. Wikipedia. *Skaftafell*. 2022 https://en.wikipedia.org/wiki/Skaftafell

erful enough to destroy a bridge. We stopped to look at part of the wreckage, twisted steel beams on the side of the road.

While the ice-covered mountains toward the center of the island were always tall and imposing, we continued to see evidence of how temporary the geography of the southern coast was. Most of it is black, sandy plains created by ash and lava, carved through with small rivers and streams. Sometimes the water spread wide like thirsty tree roots, other times they carved a channel. More than once, we crossed a bridge that used to span a steady stream but now only arched across an ash/soil/sand mix. Everywhere, the ground looked soft. As if with each step my foot would sink and water would rush in to leak into my shoes.

Most eruptions, and their debris, flood south to the sea and I remembered our food tour guide explaining how frequent eruptions had gotten in the way of Iceland developing a thriving, diverse range of plants. In those black, sandy areas, nothing grew. I didn't even see weeds.

These plains can be tricky to cross, so it's always good to check the weather, but their ability to become dangerous quickly I'm sure played into why off-roading is illegal in the country. Just like you wouldn't enter a slot canyon when there's a risk of rain, don't travel in the area surrounding a volcano if there are reports of seismic activity. Even if there's no spewing lava, melted glacier water rushing to the ocean can be deadly.

***

Vatnajökull National Park is divided into four cardinal areas – North, South, East, and West. We were taken to an area in the south called Skatafell. In 1968, Skaftafell had been declared a national park, but upon the creation of Vatnajökull National Park in 2018, it got absorbed and is now considered a part of Vatnajökull. The area has been described as similar to the Alps, something I can't confirm having never been to the Alps, and is known for having sunny days in summer - an uncommon thing in south Iceland.[5] Its three highlights are a valley, Morsárdalur, a mountain, Kristínartindar, and Skaftafellsjökull, an outlet glacier of Vatnajökull.

Our hike was on a neighboring outlet glacier called Falljökull. We started the tour by gearing up, our guide checking everyone's shoes. He eyed mine with a slight furrow, before declaring them an okay but not great option for the hike and left it up to me if I wanted to rent a pair. Vikki, to her dismay, had been outright told that no, her shoes would not work.

She whined. She'd bought them specifically for this trip, and the staff at REI had ensured her they should work. Still, off she went to rent an appropriate pair. She was still happy with the shoes she'd bought; they were comfortable and worked well for hikes. It didn't stop me from feeling bad; I was the one who made her go out and buy new shoes in the first place.

Everyone got outfitted with crampons, a metal frame of spikes that we would attach to the bottom of our shoes, helmets, ice picks, and safety harnesses. There were mutterings of us being tied in a line, but we were reassured the harnesses only served as emergency handholds for would-be rescuers. We all hoped they wouldn't be needed.

Glacier hikes rarely start on the ice. They're too protected, and at times too unpredictable. Instead, you hike to the foot of the ice. Our

---

5. Wikipedia. *Skaftafell*. 2022 https://en.wikipedia.org/wiki/Skaftafell

guide pointed out small plants and explained the short-term history of the glacier as we went along.

Glaciers *move*. It might be hard to believe, they're so large, but they are impacted by gravity just like the rest of the world. Very slowly, ice flows from the top of the ice cap down toward the sea. They push the earth as they go, forming ridges of stone and cliffs the way your foot does when you slide in gravelly sand.

As a result, glaciers are frequently bordered by rocks and cliffs that shed. Bottom sections of glaciers can be covered in a layer of stones and mud. Falljökull was covered enough it looked like a mud-splattered dog, rolling down between tall cliffs.

The dirt layer acts as insulation, but not enough to stop the glacier from melting. Our guide pointed to the lagoon at the front of the glacier. The water was muddy, uninviting to even birds. Lagoons, he explained, only exist when a glacier is shrinking. The ice heading toward the ocean lost enough mass that it retreated, leaving meltwater trapped behind the rims of earth it created pushing forward. The lagoon gets bigger the further the glacier retreats, meltwater filling the space.

I know climate change is real, and I blame Chicago being 70F in late October on that profusely, but there's a difference between noting shifting weather patterns and seeing something as large as a glacier disappear.

Falljökull's lagoon didn't exist 20 years ago.

Iceland is watching the backbone of its country die. They even held a funeral for the glacier Okjökull in 2019,[6] though it had been declared dead in 2014.[7]

That said, Falljökull is unique in how it's reacted to climate change. Glaciers usually respond in one of three ways – melt in place, shrink, or sublimate so that the ice turns into water vapor, bypassing the liquid stage.[8] Falljökull is doing something different.

It stopped moving between 2004 and 2006 and developed a fault line.[9] The British Geological Survey likened it to a lizard dropping its tail because the glacier is healthy and flowing on the top; ice slides down and over the fault to collide with the stationary ice below. The result is a glacier that acts healthy, even if it's downsized considerably. This behavior was noticed in 2014, recent in terms of geology, but it provides hope of glaciers surviving in some capacity the rising temperatures.

---

6. ABC News Australia. *Sacred Landscapes: solastalgia and spirituality in a melting world.* Meredith Lake, Karen Tong, Jennifer Parsonage and Ann-Marie Debettencor. 2021 https://www.abc.net.au/radionational/programs/soul-search/sacred-landscapes:-solastalgia-and-spirituality-in-a-melting-wo/13763576

7. NASA Earth Observatory. *Okjökull Remembered.* Kathryn Hansen. 2019 https://earthobservatory.nasa.gov/images/145439/okjokull-remembered

8. Smithsonian Magazine. *This Glacier in Iceland Is Fighting to Stay Alive.* Maris Fessenden. 2014 https://www.smithsonianmag.com/smart-news/glacier-iceland-fighting-stay-alive-180953107/

9. Advancing Earth and Space Science Blogosphere. *Health check reveals how glacier is declining due to warming climate.* Lauren Noakes. 2014 https://blogs.agu.org/geospace/2014/10/13/health-check-reveals-glacier-declining-due-warming-climate/

Falljökull translates to 'falling glacier' because the upper, active portion resembles a waterfall. It's a series of jagged peaks tumbling down, and our guide was adamant that it *was* falling. As we approached the pebbly base, he called out a large rocky scar. Two weeks ago, an icefall had exposed the mountainside. There used to be a small ice cave he liked to show off, but that'd been gone for two months. And the jagged, frozen rapids up top would be smoothed-out waves in the area tours explored in a manner of months.

We were only safe on the glacier because we would be hiking on familiar, constantly surveyed ice. Glacier hiking is something people can do alone, just like mountaineering, but there's a training process for it in Iceland covering not just how to use an ice pick and read maps, but also knowing, and predicting, the ice.

He yanked on his harness loops, and the idea of them being emergency handholds made a lot more sense. Cracks could form under our feet, sending us tumbling into the glacier. "Travel in a single file line," our guide said, "And don't go where I tell you not to."

The foot of the glacier was dirty, layers of dirt and stone providing enough traction we didn't need the crampons. We carried them looped through our ice pick handles, the metal clanking. The sun beat down on us for a rare sunny day, warming our hands even as it encouraged the creation of melt streams. They snaked through the muddy top layer, a constant reminder my footing was shifting; not a comforting thought when walking up a slope.

Once we were on top of the glacier, we gathered in a circle and put on our crampons. With the spikes on my feet, I found it hard to walk in my normal heel-to-toe fashion. Instead, I fell into a clomping, flatfooted gait similar to when I wear ski boots. Only the heavy pressure of my steps was a purposeful effort to dig the spikes into ice rather than the force of gravity on a 5 lb plastic shoe.

Mom was so excited to be on a glacier, looking up at the falling ice as we navigated through rolling, narrow hills of ice. The hills ranged from six to eight feet, so we never felt dwarfed. Ice melt streams were everywhere, and our guide liked to point toward small hollows full of clear water. These pockets were often the result of a sunbaked stone sinking through the ice or an indication that under our feet was a stream of water flowing out to the lagoon. Glaciers, surprisingly, aren't solid all the way through. There are pockets of air and water, a result of shifting as the glacier moves.

At one point, we heard a *crack*. As one, twenty of us looked skyward, but we couldn't see anything. Ice fracturing, our guide said. Another indication that a glacier is an always moving, sleeping threat.

Still, they seem safer than sand dunes. There's one not that far from me that famously swallowed a child in 2013. [10] He survived and Mount Baldy is now closed to foot traffic[11] while glaciers continue to host tours.

Our glacier guide led us to a wide run-off stream he invited us to drink from. Glacier water is pure, especially if it comes from the center of the glacier where it hasn't been dirtied by mud and stones.

---

10. Smithsonian Magazine. *They Mystery of Why This Dangerous Sand Dune Swallowed A Boy*. Ariel Sabar. Dec 2014 https://www.smithsonianmag.com/science-nature/mystery-why-dangerous-sand-dune-swallowed-boy-180953404/

11. Chicago Tribune. *Boy's rescue remembered as 'Miracle on Mount Baldy'*. Colleen Mastony. Sept 14, 2014. https://www.chicagotribune.com/news/ct-miracle-mount-baldy-met-20140914-story.html

He placed his ax across the stream and used it as a grip bar, slowly lowering himself into a push-up to drink hands-free from the water. Michele, shameless, asked him to do it again while she watched his butt. She might be almost retired and would never make a move, but she frequently admired the forms of good-looking guys. When we shared photos later, Vikki inquired about a photo of a restaurant cook and Michele just laughed, saying he was handsome.

I passed on glacial water, but Vikki tried. "Cold," was all she said, and I can't imagine what else it would taste like. A hint of lemon?

We lingered on an ice plain, for lack of a better word. The ice was flat, compared to the slopes we'd been climbing. Our guide made sure to keep an eye on us and wasn't above telling someone to come closer as we spread out to take photos. He mentioned it was a safety thing, and I wonder if that was where the active part of Falljökull pushed over the fault separating it from the dead ice. If so, I'm glad he didn't tell us directly. I would not have had the confidence to swing my ice pick over my should and cock my hip for a photo.

Mom and Michele asked for photos aplenty, arms raised in joy. "We're on a glacier!" they shouted while I snapped a picture. Vikki, in contrast, went looking for glam shots. Still, our group photo was all smiles as we smooshed together, helmets touching.

Our time on the glacier was brief but enjoyable; the weather cooperated to give us sun and blue skies the entire time. I stamped my crampons to hear the crunch of ice under the metal, and Vikki kept finding new ice slopes to pose in front of.

We hit a steep slope on our return, forcing our guide to descend first and etch out footholds with his ax. We went down one by one, placing the head of the ax on the slope for a balance aid, leaning far back to counteract gravity. Shaved ice similar to what you'd see in a snow cone collected at the bottom of the steep hill.

"Does it hurt the ice?" one of the older Australian women asked. "Having hikers on it?"

"Not really," the glacier guide answered. He scratched at the ice we walked. "We're only disturbing the snow crust, which refreshes every day or so as the glacier melts. Us on here today doesn't hurt the glacier."

We could all hear the 'but' and he opened up about the construction done to make the glacier accessible. He'd mentioned earlier an ice cave he'd liked to take people to, now unsafe as the glacier shifted. It had been such an attraction his employer planned to burrow into the ice to create a bigger, more impressive cave. Hollowing a part of the glacier, he said, *would* hurt it.

"It's not the people, but the industry." He shook his head, helping us take off our crampons as we entered the muddy part of the glacier. I couldn't help but recall hikes I'd done in Ethiopia. They were wild treks, including one moment where we spotted a pack of hyenas, but they were also so beautiful and immersive because there was no hint of civilization. Tourism exists in Ethiopia, but not where I spent two years. There had been nothing preventing cactuses from growing over paths or furthering the erosion of mountain stone.

I'm surprised that Iceland, for being so ecologically conscious, has no visitor quotas I'm aware of. Parts of the United States certainly do, with people applying to the lotto for Coyote Bluff for years before getting lucky. Maybe the country relies too much on tourism to risk it.

Jökulsárlón Glacier Lagoon

Jökulsárlón Glacier Lagoon is a picturesque spot, flowing into the equally famous Diamond Beach. My first time in Iceland, it had been my favorite location. There's nothing else like it; the reflective water, the floating chunks of blue glacier ice, the polished pieces of crystal on shore.

Michele was excited for this place. Her research for the trip had been photography spots, and in terms of stunning photos Glacier Lagoon was top three, easy. "We'll start on the beach, and then as we walk to the lagoon the ice will get bigger and bigger," she explained.

I nodded, already familiar with what we'd find, and left the group behind to amble toward shore at a slower pace. A combination of slight nausea from our back-of-the-bus seats and my introverted nature made me want to break away for a little while, even if it was only five minutes.

Nearly ten years ago, I'd taken a road trip with my sister and mother. We started in Detroit, then made our way to the Outer Banks, hitting sights along the way. We were in each other's pockets all day, every day, and I remember day three or four sitting in a restaurant booth stubbornly refusing to talk to them. They kept pressuring me, what was wrong, why wasn't I talking, and I claimed a headache.

In reality, I was just tired of sharing space with them. But I had to be there. It was dinner time, humans need food, and the idea of eating by myself in a strange place felt silly. I wanted them gone, or me gone, and the feeling didn't go away after a night's rest. I begged off going to the beach that day, saying I'd stay in the hotel. I sat in a chair in the corner of our room and read a book for hours, and when my sister and mother walked back in ready for lunch my introvert batteries were charged. I could socialize again.

I'd warned Vikki prior to our trip: my introverted ways were going to crop up at some point and she shouldn't feel like she'd done something wrong. It was just me needing solo time. She was good about it, especially the nights when I sat journaling in a corner while the others chatted. On the bus between locations, with drives taking anywhere from fifteen minutes to two hours, she also didn't disturb me. I think those peaceful bus moments were the reason why I didn't feel the intense need for solo time on the trip; I got it in little doses the whole week and a half. Still,t I needed just a bit extra that afternoon.

Diamond Beach is a black sand beach, like many on the island. It's smoothed down basalt from lava flows. What makes Diamond

Beach, or Breiðamerkursandur as it's called locally[1], special is what washes up on the sand. It's a common resting stop for iceberg chunks and the contrast between clear ice and black sand is stunning.

That day, the beach was covered in small to mid-sized chunks of ice, none larger than a terrier, though solid pieces of blue ice six feet tall have swept onto shore. I walked along the beach, shoes sinking into the sand, and picked a favorite ice chunk or two for a close-up photo. Each piece was glass-clear, truly reminiscent of diamonds. There were other tourists on the beach, but none of us moved the ice for photo posing. Some things you can only look at.

Michele, Mom, and Vikki arrived, snapping photos while I felt the urge to move. Diamond Beach sits at the mouth of Jökulsárlón, so I ambled toward it. Michele joined me, marveling over the ice. We were entering the Golden Hour, as photographers call it. It's the time before sunset, or sunrise if you're up early enough, where daylight is redder and softer than normal, giving everything a golden glow.

The closer we got to the lagoon, roughly a quarter mile away, the larger the chunks of ice bobbing in the water became. And then, in the lagoon itself, floated things I can honestly only describe as icebergs. Technically an iceberg has to be more than 50 ft long to be called as such, smaller pieces are called growlers or bergy bits[2], but I'm sure a few in the lagoon were that big.

---

1. Guide to Iceland. *Iceland Has Got a sparkling Ice Diamond Beach on Breiðam erkursandur.* Regína Hrönn Ragnarsdóttir. 2023 https://guidetoiceland.is/connect-with-locals/regina/iceland-s-diamond-beach

2. Wikipedia. *Iceberg.* 2023 https://en.wikipedia.org/wiki/Iceberg

Each piece of ice used to belong to Breiðamerkurjökull. Unlike the glacier we'd hiked earlier that day, which ended on earth with its meltwater extending beyond the glacier to form a lagoon, Breiðamerkurjökull stretches over the water on the lagoon's northwest side. The ice calves, or breaks off from the glacier, and falls into the water to slowly begin melting. When it's small enough, the bergy bit escapes the lagoon by flowing under the Road No 1 bridge to start its oceanic journey. Sometimes it returns to Diamond Beach as a washed-up ice chunk: much smaller but see-through and polished.

The ice in the lagoon isn't clear. Much of it is white with dark streaks that give the ice a marble look, the result of trapped dirt or volcanic ash.[3] Occasionally you'll get a ribbon of blue, which is a sign that the ice lacks any air bubbles that can distort light. Much of the ice floating in the lagoon has this blue undertone, hinting at how dense the inside of the ice is and how old. It takes time and pressure to push out air.

Ice wasn't the only thing swimming in the water. Michele excitedly gestured to movement, and we found ourselves watching seals. I kept expecting one to jump out of the water to bask on the ice, but none did. Perhaps that's a left-over false expectation from watching the seals at Pier 39 when I lived in San Francisco, or maybe sunset was too close for sunbathing, or the weather too cold. Despite being one of the better weather days the whole trip, it was also chilly and I'd

---

3. Nordic Visitor Blog. *Diamond Beach in Iceland: Your Complete Guide.* Camila. 2022 https://www.nordicvisitor.com/blog/diamond-beach-attraction-guide-iceland/

tried my best to stop heat loss. I'm wearing a hat in our photos at Jökulsárlón despite how awkward the beret-wannabe looked.

While we watched the seals, Vikki and Mom caught up and we continued along the lagoon's edge. The closer we got to the glacier, the bigger the ice chunks were, and the more likely we were to see the turquoise blue of pure ice. We picked up pieces of clear ice we found on the shore, displaying our new diamond earrings or a diamond tiara.

"You need someone to get you a ring this big, Ginny," Michele jibbed, pointing out an ice chunk larger than my hand.

"Yeah," Mom joined in. "And make sure the guy is cute like our glacier guide."

I rolled my eyes. I was the only single woman, of course, they'd make such jokes. I let them slide, but I find such things tiresome. As an ace woman, I don't have the same approach or desire toward a partner they had, and I don't feel a strong need for companionship. While Vikki and my mother knew my orientation, Michele did not. It had zero impact on our relationship. She did not need to know, other than knowing.

Coming out as ace to the older generation – anyone over 40 I'd say – is just plain daunting because I cannot say "I'm ace" and leave it at that. It's so unfamiliar a term, even to parts of the queer community despite being decades old, that coming out often involves an education lesson. I didn't want to go through all that with Michele, especially not on vacation and low on social batteries.

"I'm gonna lick it," Vikki said, picking up the ice chunk.

Sometimes, that's the best thing an ally can do. Notice their friend is experiencing a microaggression and turn the conversation around.

I laughed, snapping a photo of Vikki with her tongue out. The 'diamond' was as big as her head.

Heading back to the bus, we came across Nathan. Still needing a slight break from people who had been in my pocket for days, I caught up to him and we chatted walking back. It was nice traveling in a big group; there were plenty of people to talk to and most of us were easy-going enough that conversations weren't hard to keep going. The exception was an older couple, weathered in a way that spoke of frequent, long outdoor adventures. I never even said hello to them.

Nathan was the youngest on the trip and the only serviceman. He didn't mind flying planes, he said, but had signed up for the Navy for the college money. He'd sparked several conversations with bus mates about their careers, getting a feel for not just the job but also the lifestyle it might provide. It was obvious he loved the thrill of visiting new places, and with four on the bus in one-income households, he had lots of questions.

Unlike the night before, we made it to the hotel before dark. Staying on a sheep farm, our tour guide recommended the lamb burger. I can't recall if the burgers came from sheep living on the farm or not, but it had been delicious.

There were two types of diners that night – those who left early to nap and those who lingered in an attempt to stay awake and make time pass. Tonight was the first of the trip with enough aurora activity to see, and everyone was eager for the chance.

Aurora Hunting

Vikki and I discussed our game plan. Auroras were at the top of our list of things to see, and with expected peak activity between 11 pm and 1 am, did we want to stay up or not?

Regardless, we wanted a glass of wine. We'd opened a bottle before dinner, and while the screw top *might* make it safe in our bags the next day we didn't want to take the risk. Time to kill it. As we poured, someone knocked. I expected 'the Moms' as Vikki had taken to calling Michele and my mother, but it was Nathan. Half the rooms in the hall were filled with our bus, but we were the first in line.

"Wanna check the sky for the aurora?"

We begged off. We'd just poked our heads outside on the walk over from the restaurant and had just decided we'd make an early night of it, setting a pre-dawn alarm. Radar didn't predict clear skies until after 1 am, after geomagnetic activity fell below visibility levels, but there was a chance to see it before sunrise. We gave Nathan a glass of wine to keep him warm as he stared at the sky. He promised if he saw the aurora, he'd text the bus Whatsapp group and knock on our door.

No knock came, but we checked more time before getting ready for bed. No aurora, but I saw more stars than I had in a while.

We came back inside, chilled but awake, and decided to check again at the top of the hour. We settled in a pair of wing-backed armchairs in a small lounge near a door, finishing our wine. From a nearby staircase, voices floated down from another group making periodic checks.

Before the hour, Nathan came down. He'd been checking every fifteen minutes, eager to see the northern lights. Vikki waggled her eyes when he joined us for our check, and she left the two of us outside as I compared New Zealand to Iceland. The countries have very similar topologies, created by active geothermal areas. Iceland has more glaciers, however. And of course, the stars are different. There's no Southern Cross in Iceland, but it was very easy to find both Dippers.

Nathan bid me goodnight at eleven-thirty. Not super late, but after a day of hiking I wanted the extra sleep. I stepped into my room to the sound of Vikki slapping product on her face. Her morning and night routine took thirty minutes.

I'd slipped into PJs and under the covers with a book when Michele invited us to look at the sky with her. Now that my feet were up, I was disinclined to move. Twenty minutes later, she texted again. The aurora had arrived.

I jumped out of bed, pulling on my coat over my PJs. I knocked on the bathroom door, letting Vikki know about Michele's message, and jogged outside.

Michele had set up at the edge of the parking lot, disregarding her DSL to take photos with her phone. I looked up at the sky and saw the same thing I'd seen earlier. Dark skies, with a faint silver cloud reflecting moonlight.

"Where is it?" I asked.

"It's that silver bit," she said and hastened to explain away my confusion.

The silver cloud in the sky wasn't reflected moonlight. Auroras aren't visible to the naked eye.[1] Not in the way I expected. To see the colors, you need prolonged exposure, a minimum of five seconds, to let the camera collect more light than the human eye can. The silver whisp *was* an aurora. The evidence sat on Michele's phone, a green streak in the sky.

I texted the Whatsapp group, but only Vikki emerged. People had posted their room numbers with requests for knocks if the aurora was spotted, so I went shrieking down the hallway. "The aurora is here!" I said, rapping on doors between skips. "The aurora is here!"

Several bus members told me the next morning I'd sounded like a giddy child, which I certainly felt at the time. I was so excited to see the aurora. So amazed at the contrast between what I saw and the photos my phone took.

A handful of bus mates joined us, spread out among the parking lot. Michele, Vikki, and I huddled together as we took photos. I didn't have a tripod, so I had to hold my phone steady to avoid a

---

1. Lights over Lapland. *What Does An Aurora Look Like To The Naked Eye?* Chris Hodgson. 2019 https://lightsoverlapland.com/what-does-an-aurora-look-like-to-the-naked-eye/

blurry photo. Even as my lips trembled in the cold, I kept my hands still as I took photo after photo, watching the aurora shift and change between shots. My early ones were just pale green fuzzy brushes, but as the night went on the green got brighter and the aurora began to dance. We could sorta see the dance with our eyes, a jagged split in the silver light, but on our cameras were two crisp lines of green arching through the sky, color bleeding up like watercolors. There was a flare, and I captured a headlight bright green glow in the middle of a streak.

Eventually, the cold overcame my excitement. My PJs weren't warm, and I couldn't operate my camera with gloves. I cocooned myself in bed. Vikki slipped into the room smiling soon after, saying the aurora had died down.

I had been worried – had an even better shot, a better aurora appeared as soon as I left? – and knowing it hadn't was a relief. I hadn't missed out on an amazing experience because I wussed out on feeling cold.

"I can't believe we saw an aurora!" Vikki said, climbing into her side of the bed. "I hope we see more."

"I'm sure we will," I answered, looking at my most recent photo. But even if we didn't, I was enthusiastic to have seen it once.

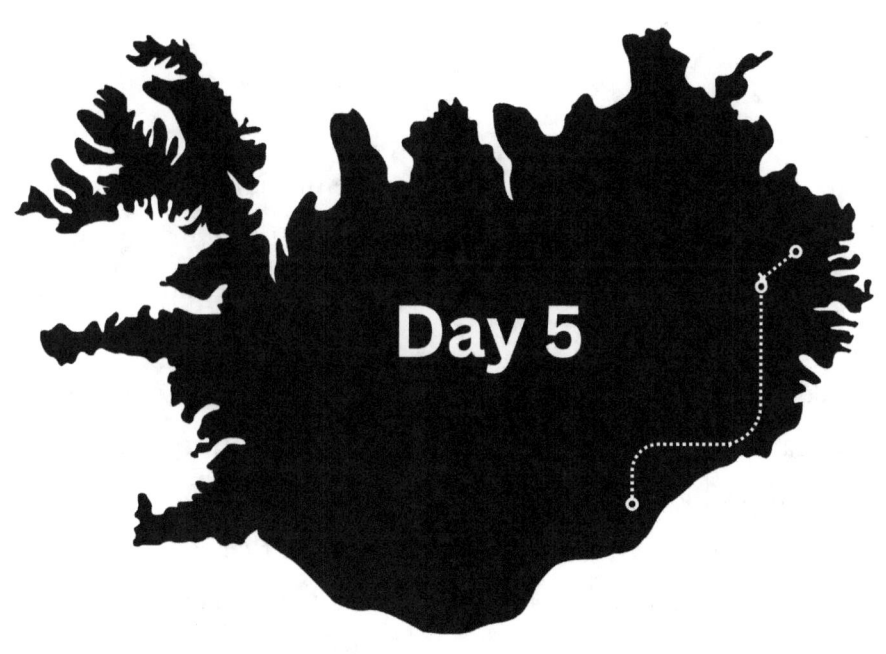

Austurland

After being regulated to the back row the previous day, Mom and Michele refused to be stuck there again. They rushed through breakfast, leaving Vikki and me to eat a variety of flavored poundcake-like bread.

Vikki and I packed last night, which meant that we had a tiny bit of extra time. She insisted we walk to the sheep pasture so she could get a sheep selfie.

The pasture our room looked out onto wasn't fenced. We crossed the parking lot and walked in a soggy car trail that followed a shallow ditch until Vikki beelined for a trio of sheep. Two white, one black, they never looked up from the grass. But two rams across the field did, heads up and watching.

I nervously looked between the rams, whose spiraled horns looked as tall as my head, and the hotel. We were out of sight, but also on private property – claimed by humans and sheep. I didn't want to incite the wrath of either. Vikki could have cared less about the farm owners, but the rams made her apprehensive. She pressed forward until her target sheep, still not looking up, headed toward the rams. She figured this was as close as she would get and took a selfie from twenty feet away.

As it turns out, farmers are pretty chill about strangers entering pastures. They must because Icelanders have a right to roam. This means people have the right to travel through private land without asking permission.[1] There are stipulations, of course. It doesn't apply to camping, so tourists who want to camp have designated campgrounds. There are some exceptions, but they're rare.[2]

There are rules to roaming: take paths whenever possible and adhere to a 'do no damage and leave no trace' principle. Many landowners put in gates or small step ladders tall enough to overcome lower fences to indicate paths. Our guide pointed out a few such step ladders later that day leading straight into sheep pastures. Vikki stared longingly out the window at them. The right to roam is restricted to foot traffic.

Iceland isn't the only country with right to roam laws; Norway, Sweden, Estonia, and Scotland are known for it.[3] The idea comes from a communal sense of land ownership, a balance between private rights and public access. It's never caught on in the States, with roaming limited to public land, but I don't have a strong desire to

---

1. Play Iceland. *Who owns Iceland? The Right to Roam in Iceland Explained.* 2023 https://playiceland.is/guide/who-owns-iceland-the-right-to-roam-in-iceland-explained/

2. Motorhome Iceland. *The Right to Roam in Iceland.* 2020 https://www.motorhomeiceland.com/post/right-to-roam-iceland

3. Right to Rome. 2023 https://www.righttoroam.org.uk/

cut across the yards in suburbia. Places like Montana used to have a public culture of the right to roam, calling it 'freedom to roam' or 'the right of responsible access', [4] but it's been fading as private landowners execute their rights. Which in America, means the right to exclude others from your property. [5]

Vikki's sadness at not getting within petting distance of sheep that morning melted away when we saw the fruit of Michele and Mom's efforts – the front row. The design of the bus, with an aisle separating paired seats on one side and single seats on the other until you got to the back bench, meant Mom and Michele sat behind our driver-cum-tour guide while Vikki and I sat behind one another in the solo seats across the aisle. I had a window seat and could make use of it because the chair wasn't elevated!

We started the day exploring a cliff top. As far as I know, there's nothing special about the overlook we stopped it. It was just a view our guide liked, easily identified by the bright red-orange lighthouse called Hvalnes. There's no lighthouse keeper, being fully automated, but we climbed its base and the surrounding areas, taking in the sight of the waves down below as they crashed onto the rocks.

The topography slowly changed. When we left Reykjavik, we traveled south on the ring road. It's flat near the coast as all volcanic eruptions flow southward to the sea, evening out the land. We'd see

---

4. Thomas J Elpel. *Freedom to Roam: Restoring the Right of Responsible Access*. Thomas J Elpel. 2020 https://thomasjelpel.wordpress.com/2020/12/17/freedom-to-roam-restoring-the-right-of-responsible-access/

5. Wikipedia. *Freedom to Roam. United States.* 2023 https://en.wikipedia.org/wiki/Freedom_to_roam#United_States

mountains and the highlands toward the center of the island, but for the most part, it was wide expanses of grass, black sand, or lava fields stretching to the ocean.

Now, we approached the east side Iceland. The ring road developed pinches and curves, and instead of being level with beaches, we found ourselves a dozen feet above them in a tame version of California's Highway 1. Our second stop of the day, a beach, had a steep, if short, decent to it from the parking lot. It was a tie if people inched down the slope, or let the momentum build for half a dozen steps to hit the large pebbles at a run. Even the beaches had become rougher, as this one had rocks half the size of my fist that knocked together as I walked on them.

The east part of the island, called Austurland[6], has scattered communities and a total population of 11,000. Many are small fishing villages, with a small reliance on tourism. It's too far for day trips from the capital, so the only people who visit are those who plan to go to the east fjords or, like our group, pass through while doing a ring tour.

We stopped for lunch in our guide's hometown, Djúpivogur. The city is a "slow movement" community,[7] cities around the world that embrace a relaxed lifestyle by eschewing things like fast food and focusing on city planning that encourages slow traffic.[8] Quality over

---

6. Visit Austruland. *About Austurland.* 2023 https://www.east.is/en/about

7. Djupivogur. *Port of Djupivogur.* 2023 https://djupivogur.is/Visit-Djupivogur/Port-of-Djupivogur/

8. Wikipedia. *Slow movement.* 2023 https://en.wikipedia.org/wiki/Slow_movement_(culture)

quantity, as supporter Carl Honoré says. If you're curious, check out the Cittaslow organization[9] which aids towns in joining the movement. There are nearly 300 of them in 33 countries, each striving for a sense of peaceful, unhurried living. I found Djúpivogur charming absolutely charming.

Forgoing a real lunch, we got coffee and split a piece of cake that was too tempting to pass up at a small café overlooking the town's harbor. It was small but large enough for one commercial fishing trawler and a dozen smaller, personal boats. They floated peacefully in the sunlight, sheltered from the larger fjord while we gazed at the mountains behind them.

From there, we headed toward the rock museum. Or as our guide knew it, Jon's house.

Jon was a retired fisherman with a long, wiry beard. At one point in his life, he wondered *why keep his rock collection to himself*? So he arranged them in his back garden and put up signs saying "Stone garden – Free Entry". We arrived to him watering his rocks with a hose.

"They're thirsty," he chuckled, aiming the stream at a rock with a large divot he'd decorated to look like a monster's face. The stream hit the back of the rock exactly, water dribbling down to wet a handful of the hundreds of rocks he'd collected.

Very social, Jon pointed out his favorite rocks. One was the size of a child's head with an extended portion that had been split down the middle. Open, it looked like a crocodile with a mouth full of crystal. His favorites were all like that – rocks that looked ordinary until they

---

9. Cittaslow. 2023 https://www.cittaslow.org/

got wet or were turned a certain way and then suddenly, there was a glittering sparkle that made him light up.

Jon collected all the rocks himself from hikes in the area, and it wasn't just rocks he brought home. Antlers. Coral from when Iceland was under the ocean. He showed us recently found rocks and described what the smallest of details meant. This banding might mean this color. A particular shape meant it'd be better to slice it vertically like dicing carrots to better display color patterns. He loved his collection, and he loved the tourists who came through. His guest book was full of people saying hi and carved into his small shop was his name in half a dozen languages.

It was the perfect retirement, he said. Having strangers from all over the world stop by to say hello and listen to him talk about his hobbies. He insisted on a photo with us, standing half a head taller than me and almost able to hold all four of us within his extended arms. "Such beautiful ladies!"

After lunch, we headed to a local secret - Foal Fall, or Folaldafoss. I found this to be one of the more charming waterfalls of the trip. The hike to it was pleasant, and while the waterfall isn't large, 55ft is still tall enough to be impressive and pretty. The waterfall feeds a small pool that quickly widens and flows through several boulders, creating a ton of nooks and crannies to explore while allowing us to get close to the bottom of the falls. It was the type of low-key, quiet area I could have easily spent hours at, dangling my toes into sun-dappled water while I read a book.

Our guide pointed out wild berry bushes and encouraged us to snack on the hike back. They were smaller than blueberries but had a similar color. I couldn't resist picking some, sharing with Vikki who gave me a purple flower for my hair in return. They were sweeter than I expected, and I collected and ate at least two handfuls.

Berry hunting made us slow, and Vikki took the opportunity to tease me about the conversations I had with Nathan yesterday, genuinely curious if they were my ace way of flirting even as she insinuated he might like me. I told her no, I was just talking to him like I'd talk to other travelers. But Nathan *did* have a habit of starting those conversations. The idea it might be his way of showing interest crept up on me in mild horror. I didn't *want* to be someone Nathan wanted to flirt with. I wasn't on vacation to flirt. And that had nothing to do with our nine-year difference. I stopped to clear a rock out of my shoe, and Vikki let the conversation drop.

One of the reasons Folaldafoss isn't very well known, despite its loveliness, is the road it's on. While technically a shortcut that bypasses a few coastal cities to save forty miles of driving,[10] Route 939 is unpaved and steep with an average gradient of 17%.[11] We went slow and steady as our guide talked about the road. He used to travel it back and forth to high school, as Djúpivogur had none, leaving the dorms on occasional weekends. The minibus handled it well enough, moving slowly as our guide babbled about being happy we were driving an official road and not just a locally forged truck path as he recalled it. If it was winter, we wouldn't have taken that route.

---

10. World Waterfall Database. *Folaldafoss*. 2023 https://www.worldwaterfalldatabase.com/waterfall/Folaldafoss-14421

11. Hiking the World. *Folaldafoss – A Remote Waterfall In a Barren Landscape*. 2023 https://hikingtheworld.blog/waterfalls/folaldafoss/

While we didn't stop to explore anything else, we passed tons of small waterfalls formed by glacier meltwater traveling to the nearest fjord. It wasn't long after we traded the dirt road for a paved one that we came to our main attraction of the day.

Hengifoss, The Hanging Falls.

The Hanging Falls

Hengifoss is the second-highest waterfall in Iceland, with water dropping 400 ft. Unlike Folaldafoss, which was a thirty-minute hike from the bus, we were given two and a half hours to hike to Hengifoss and back for a total three-mile hike.

Hengifoss is on private land and fenced off, but thanks to the right to roam the public, including tourists, have access. A large gate announced the start of a well-worn path over the first green hill. Vikki got excited at the sign asking us to make sure the gate stayed closed to keep the sheep in, but we only ever saw white dots in the distance.

The walk started with an even, but very noticeable incline. Despite this being our second hike of the day, I was energized and kept hurrying ahead. I ran out to an outlook and back, hoping for a view but told the group they could skip it. Vikki and I forged ahead, her huffing to keep up. She's six inches shorter than me and most of my height is in my legs. I frequently make use of it with large strides.

To the left, the ground dropped away into a river gorge. The water didn't take up the full width of the bottom as the river wove around rocks and tumbled over small cascades. It was too far away to hear it, but every peak over the edge of the hill revealed sun-gleaming water and spots of white froth.

We came across a lesser waterfall, Litlanesfoss, that poured out of the rocks surrounded by chipped-off hexagonal basalt pillars that were becoming a common sight. Waterfalls as a whole were becoming common.

"Another one?" asked one of the young Australian women on the tour. "I can't believe I'm saying this, but I'm getting sick of waterfalls."

There were muddled comments of similar opinions. While our only second up-close waterfall of the day, it was maybe the seventh we'd seen. Three days into this ring tour, I wouldn't be surprised if our count was close to twenty waterfalls if you included all the small ones we'd seen from the bus or in the distance from some of our hikes.

I didn't share the waterfall fatigue. I love them, and during COVID took a solo road trip across Michigan's Upper Peninsula to hit eleven of them in a week. So while not tired of waterfalls, I had turned picky over which ones I liked and deemed worth a photo.

Litlanesfoss is one I ignored. I took one photo, and the fall was shadowed. Maybe it would have looked better in morning light or closer to noon when the tall cliffs of the gorge weren't blocking sunlight. Or in the summer when it would have a stronger flow. But to this waterfall chaser, it's okay to miss it.

The path evened out and we transitioned from walking on top of highland hills, watching the wind blow through tall grasses, to walking into a wide box canyon whose large cliffs cast the trail in shadow. The grass disappeared and we walked on rocks to look up at smooth strata. I was unexpectedly reminded of the American Southwest, except the colors were wrong. Where Arizona and Utah are filled with gold and pink and red, there was nothing here but shades of gray and brown. That's because the rocks are different – Iceland's strata are red clay pressed between basalt lava rock instead of the sandstone common in the Southwest.[1]

Eventually, the ground became uneven enough a wooden walkway had been built to prevent a scramble. It was hard to tell how old the installation was, the wood looked in good repair but at least one rockslide had damaged it. We walked around two small boulders, their weight enough to warp the wood.

And then, there it was. Hengifoss. It fell at the end of the box canyon, hugging the stone cliff to presumably fill a pool. We couldn't see the bottom, it was hidden behind a mound of gravel, but the trail dead end at a bend in the river created by Hengifoss's flow. Scattered with large rocks, Vikki and I hopped from one to another to explore the area without getting our shoes wet.

In a future trip where I can hike on my timeline, I'd love to pick my way through the river rocks and scramble to the bottom of Hengifoss. It looked doable, especially with good shoes, and later research revealed there's a cave behind the flow you can access and a pile of

---

1. Cars Island. *Hengifoss Waterfall: Hike and Travel Tips* 2020 https://www.carsiceland.com/post/hengifoss-waterfall

collapsed sandstone, rare for Iceland.[2] But that afternoon, I was okay finding two rocks to wedge myself between and relax, listening to the shallow river run by.

"Hello, girls!" Mom waved from the wooden platform at the end of the trail. Michele sat on a bench, but Mom rock-stepped to join Vikki and me. "We made it," she said with a big grin.

Mom loves "making it". Every hike to a view was a success to celebrate with a group photo and a moment to take in the scenery. From Kentucky's Red River Gorge to the hike from Fira to Oia on Santorini to this hike to Hengifoss, each is an adventure Mom was proud of achieving.

I used to share her enthusiasm as a child, but it's faded as I've gotten older. I'm probably, sadly, too experienced a traveler. I *know* I can make it. But as Mom sat on a big rock, taking the time to breathe, and Michele sat on the bench with her knee brace on, I wondered if Mom's enthusiasm for each hike had shifted. No longer encouragement and joy for her daughter, but praise and joy for herself. "Making it" might not be a guarantee in ten years. We'd already changed one vacation plan in the past five to align with her physical fitness.

But that hike? That hike Mom made.

When we turned back, Vikki and I again abandoned Michele and Mom to their slower pace. At the base of the hike was a small hut selling sheep's milk ice cream. We hoped to get down first and use

---

2. Guide to Iceland. *The Majestic Hengifoss and Litlanesfoss Waterfalls in East Iceland.* Regína Hrönn Ragnarsdóttir. 2023 https://guidetoiceland.is/connect-with-locals/regina/hengifoss-waterfall-in-east-iceland

the extra time to make the purchase, giving the Moms the maximum amount of ice cream eating time.

Vikki and I ran into hikers going in the other direction near the beginning of the box canyon. The walls cast long shadows on the trail, and the river at this point was a long drop below instead of the flat water we'd played in. The trail was single file, so to get out of the way of the hikers comping up I stepped to the right. This put me further away from the rim of the gorge, only inches away, but also took me off the trail and onto a slope of loose gravel.

The first hiker passed. I took a second step. My foot slipped. The second hiker's face went white, and I'm sure mine did too as I imagined us tumbling over stones to the river fifty feet below.

He made an aborted movement toward me, even as to regain my balance I turned my downward motion into forward motion. I took a large step forward, passing the second hiker and praying for a more stable spot as I removed weight from my sliding back foot. I took another step, a crab cross onto the flat, solid trail. I stayed there for half a second, arms still out for balance, and felt my heart pound against my sternum.

I moved forward, giving Vikki room to maneuver, but not looking back. I don't know how she passed the other hikers, but I heard her steps behind me.

I continued, heartbeat calming, but knowing I had avoided a disastrous fall. Twenty steps later I reached a wide area and Vikki was immediately at my side asking if I was okay. While I had only glimpsed the man's face, she'd gotten a full look at his terror and imagined us going over the cliff as well. Her fear soothed my own as I concentrated on calming her down.

New hiking shoes went on the Christmas list.

We crossed a bridge, and I resolutely didn't look down into the gorge. We now hiked on the opposite side of the river we'd hiked up, once again in sunlight and surrounded by tall, fall grasses. We noticed Nathan standing on an outcropping, and Vikki nudged me to go talk to him. She wore a match-making grin. I flipped her off before checking out the view Nathan found, leaving Vikki to take a photo of a flower.

Mom and Michele made good time, catching up to the three of us. We turned into a leap-frogging group of five, depending on who had stopped for photos and conversations. At one point, Mom turned to me with mock upset. "Vikki said you swore at her."

"Vikki!" I shouted to where she walked ahead further down the hill. "Tattletale!"

She laughed, and in the middle, Michele looked back at us. "Siblings," she said. "They always tell."

I hid my laughter behind a false frown. A mutual friend's mother-in-law had called us sisters once, a true testament to how well Vikki and I get along. Sometimes I feel like different friends know different mes – who I am with my Dungeons & Dragons group is different from who I am with my Peace Corps friends is different from who I am with my writing community or ace community. Sometimes I blur them, just a bit at the edge.

From what I want in a relationship to my current media obsession, I can trust Vikki with anything. We've ranted to each other, provided shelter when needed. I taught her how to drive a car, she helped me learn to code. She's helped me navigate dating, and I've witnessed the rough sides of her marriage.

I considered her my Chicago sister before, but her tattling on me and conspiring with Mom went beyond that. She isn't *like* a sister, she *is* a sister.

I have no complaints. Mom and Vikki had already halfway adopted each other. In previous trips to Chicago, Mom had encouraged me to invite Vikki to dinner after work and Vikki could use a positive mother figure in her life.

This is a standard occurrence with my mother. When I left for college, one of the things she was sad about was losing status as the 'hang out house' and thus no longer able to interact with not just me, but my gaggle of friends. Last Easter, she invited one of my college friends to join us for dinner. She and her husband didn't even bat an eye at the two-hour drive.

We finished the hike with achy feet, more than ready for that ice cream. I was worried about time but tossed my concern out the window when I noticed others in our group in the early stages of their snack. If we weren't the only stranglers, our guide would give us the extra time.

Grabbing a few half pints, not just sheep ice cream but the normal kind from cow milk as well, I joined my vacation family at a wooden booth in the sun. Sheep ice cream, as it turns out, is not something I would know is made from sheep if we hadn't taste-tested it against regular ice cream. It was a little fattier, but not much. I'd certainly eat it again.

Mom stole my wooden spoon, so I snagged Vikki's, laughing, while Michele leaned back with a sigh.

"This was a good hike," she said.

"It was!" Mom said, handing me back my spoon. "It'd be better with a beer at the end though."

"We still have wine in our suitcase," Vikki offered.

"It's okay," Michele said. "We'll just drink at the hotel."

Evening Searches

We got to the hotel before the end of happy hour. Fitting for a hotel named after one of Odin's halls. Everyone scurried to dump their suitcases in the bedrooms before heading to the bar. BOGO wine was on everyone's mind.

While the wine selection in Reykjavik contained brands and labels I understood, this bar's selection was foreign to me. It's not like I expected California wines, the import costs would be huge, but I did expect to find varieties I was familiar with. In reality, not a single wine on the menu was something I'd heard of and a good deal of them were Argentinian. I found this surprising; it's not like France is *that* far away from Iceland and the quality of English wines has been improving.[1] Despite the oddity, I didn't mind; it was simply another adventure of the trip.

---

1. Robb Report. *'We're One of the Very Few Winners in a World Full of Losers': How English Wine is Benefiting From Climate Change.* Ben Oliver. Feb, 5th, 2023 https://robbreport.com/food-drink/wine/england-vineyards-benefitting-climate-change-1234797738/

Sadly, I barely got to touch it before bad luck struck. The four of us found a small sitting area, a couch and two armchairs sharing a low coffee table. Eight glasses of wine wouldn't fit, but if we held our current drinks in hand we got by. The problem came when Mom pulled the table closer to her. The glasses wobbled, and my second glass of wine spilled all over my lap and into the upholstery of my seat.

It was a lot of wine, and it was hard to concentrate on my mother's apology when I could feel it seeping into my underwear. I stood up, saying for the third time it was alright. It's just wine. These aren't good clothes. I had more worry for the chair. Staff came to help clean, and I left them to it. I scurried down to the hotel room to shower.

That night was the only one I did laundry the whole trip, using a soap bar to scrub everything I'd been wearing. T-shirt. Undershirt. Pants. Underwear. I rounded out the collection with several of my sports bras, using every inch of the shower wall and room radiator to dry my rough attempt at laundry.

Squeaky clean, I took the opportunity to wear one of my nice tops. We had fewer occasions to wear them than expected, and if I had packed them, why not?

Mom was apologetic, sliding over replacement wine, and I took a glass in hand after claiming a new seat. Clean, beginning to relax, I was ready for dinner.

We were in an actual town that night, and an hour ago we'd been excited by having multiple dinner options. Settled in our seats, however, we decided to not move and just order from the hotel's restaurant.

Especially those first few days of the tour, before we got into the rhythm of the trip, most of us turned lethargic at the hotel. Between more daily walking than we were used to and the travel fatigue of car rides, it wasn't just our feet that ached by the end of the day. Or brains did too, busy with processing new sights and activities. Everyone became a justified lazy butt in the evening, taking the easy option. Maybe a fourth of the bus left to dine at someplace other than the hotel that night. The rest of us simply lounged in one spot or another for a few hours, physically recovering.

We perked up about nine as darkness crept in and aurora hunting invaded our minds. The weather report predicted similar aurora activity as the previous night but without pesky cloud cover. Our guide suggested the soccer field across the street as a good spot. There'd be light from the streetlights, but toward the center of the field and near the bleachers it would be dark enough for some good shots.

Vikki and I bundled up in coats, neck warmers, and gloves to meet Michele in the field. She lay on the grass, her tiny tripod against a goalpost, already taking photos. Vikki and I stood behind her and looked up.

We immediately spotted the sliver whisp we now knew to be the aurora. It was just as bright as the previous night, which is to say not very, but there were several silver patches in the sky. They came and went over both goalposts, and a third form was in the distance over the hotel parking lot. There were *multiple auroras*.

I ignored Vikki's look when Nathan wandered over for a chat. She was convinced he liked me, but if so, he was subtle.

I once had a guy on a bus tour in New Zealand ask my opinion on travel romances after we'd been a bus pair for a day. I thought it was an honest question and I answered a vacation was too short a time to know someone well enough to be in a relationship. Now I can say it was probably a probe about what we could physically do in the next week and I was too ace to realize it.

I have a habit of not knowing when people are hitting on me, a mix of being ace and general cluelessness. As it was, only Vikki thought there was something there, even if Mom and Michele would not be averse to encouraging such a thing.

Mom's pressuring me about dating has backed off over the years. It was highest when I was 27 and 29, the ages she got married and had me respectfully, but I know she wants me to find someone. She's concerned I'll be lonely as I age, and while I'm not, I do sometimes think about how nice it would be to have a partner to feed my cat when I'm gone for a weekend.

A roommate would do that, but a roommate wouldn't also make sure I don't skip lunch or make me soup when I'm ill. It's support I want, not sex. And certainly not sex in a hotel room with someone I barely knew.

Nathan was never anything but friendly, even side-by-side under the night sky in a situation many would label romantic. Vikki could see what she wanted in his actions toward me, but I saw nothing but a bus buddy.

Eventually, I got cold, and with roughly twenty photos on my phone, I didn't feel the need to stay out. Michele, Vikki, and I trooped back to the hotel. I eagerly changed into PJs, put a pillow under my feet, and reached for my book. Vikki took up her skincare routine when our bus chat pinged. New photos of the aurora, and at a much more active level than we'd seen yet.

I was hesitant to go out, the photos were ten minutes old and auroras shifted quickly. A thirty-second dance was long, and the concentration of green our cameras could pick up varied. It's why aurora hunting was just us pointing our cameras at the sky taking shot after shot, curious about the result.

I doubted was worth the effort to get out of bed, but Vikki pulled on pants over her pajamas. "We came here to see the aurora," she said. "I don't know if I'll ever be able to see it again."

Her words resonated, when would I see this again? I would like to. But not enough to go out in the cold and dark.

I stayed in bed. Vikki took the hotel key and left, promising to be back in thirty minutes.

Only she wasn't and I got worried. I texted, got no response, and tried to keep my cool while I bundled up. I walked through the parking lot, wishing I'd put on my neck warmer, and crossed the street to the soccer field. I couldn't see anyone, so I did a loop to no avail. I called Vikki. Texted her. And when I got no answer, returned to the hotel room. It was slightly ajar, just as I left it because we'd been given one key and Vikki had it.

She wasn't in the room.

My worry accelerated. We were in a small town, and Iceland has practically no crime. What had happened? Did she and some of the other travelers go to a nearby bar? Wander to a different spot? Had I just missed them, in the shadow of the trees surrounding the soccer field?

I went back to the field. It was empty. I lingered in the parking lot, where the aurora was currently the brightest, and snapped a few photos, sending one to Vikki as if bait to lure her to me.

Just as I entered the hotel room for a second time, I got a return text. *At the bar with the girls.*

The girls were the trio of Australian women on the trip. Each were traveling solo, but had become a unit after the first day. Drinking with them would certainly explain why Vikki hadn't seen my messages.

Like Vikki, they figured this was the only time they'd see the Northern Lights and had committed to regular checks to see if the activity had spiked. Coming inside for a break from the cold, they'd hoped to waste time at the bar only to find staff cleaning up. In a move I've never seen in America, the hotel staff served them and told them to place the glasses on the bar when they were finished. The morning crew would wash them.

I joined the group as one of the women claimed bedtime. She gave me her seat and untouched glass of wine. Just what I needed to warm up and calm down from my search for Vikki. I'd had surface conversations with the Australian women before, but alone in that corner of the bar we got to talking, blowing past the 30-minute mark to check the skies. We dived into careers and home life before gossiping about our fellow travelers. Vikki brought up Nathan.

"I think he likes Ginny," she said, but the idea was immediately shut down. The girls believed Nathan's attractions lay elsewhere – the younger of the two solo Asian-American women on the trip.

"Nathan always perks up near her. Asks her a lot of questions. Jogs up to her on hikes."

I hadn't noticed, but I felt relieved. I didn't *want* Nathan to like me, and if only Vikki thought he did, there was a higher likelihood he didn't.

We finished our drinks, then checked on the aurora. The silver wisp was so weak we didn't bother pulling out our phones. With a chorus of goodbyes, we split for our rooms. It was after 1 am at that point, and I collapsed into bed. I fluffed up my foot pillow and buried myself under the duvet.

Vikki, bless her heart, finished her skincare routine before crawling under the covers.

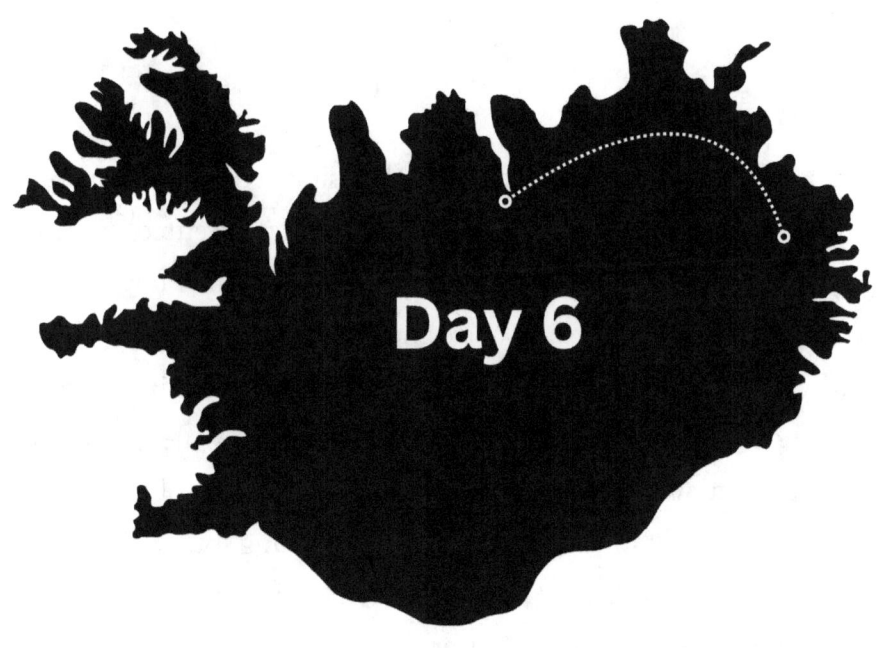

Day 6

Collapsing Waterfall

Our guide had told us only one bus rule – sit in a different seat every day – and we'd all done our best to follow it. It prevented the same people from being stuck in the back day after day but also worked to shuffle conversation partners and window views.

Michele and Mom slightly cheated the next morning – again claiming the front row – but in accordance with the rules graciously handed them over to Vikki and me. They sat in the row behind us.

We were solidly in the east fjords that morning, but we'd be out of them before the day was over. I prayed before we left we'd see something on my wishlist: reindeer.

There are wild reindeer in Iceland, despite not being native to the country. They were transplanted from Norway[1] and did okay-ish on the island. The population slowly dwindled due to poor grazing and now stays in a section of east Iceland. I'd seen reindeer in zoos and

---

1. Iceland Hotel Collection By Berjaya. *Magazine. Reindeer Run Wild in East Iceland.* 2015 https://www.icelandhotelcollectionbyberjaya.com/magazine/blog/wild-reindeer-iceland-mag

Christmas events, but I wanted to see them running free. Even if it was from the bus window.

It wasn't that far into the drive, maybe thirty minutes, that our guide called our attention to the right side of the bus. Reindeer!

He pulled over so we could get out, and all thoughts of reindeer were swept out of my head by the extreme speed of the wind. It pulled at my coat, and I instantly regretted my choice of pants. I should have gone for a more insulated pair or worn an underlayer, but I'd completely forgotten to factor in the wind when dressing for the day.

Vikki, trying to put on her coat, almost lost it. I have a great photo of her holding the ends of her coat up behind her back, the nylon puffed enough she could go parasailing.

Our arrival disrupted the reindeer. They picked up their heads and trotted away over a hill. My photo was blurry, zoomed in too far, but I didn't care. Reindeer seen with my own eyes, check! That completed my Iceland list. Spas. Glaciers. Waterfalls. The Northern Lights. Reindeer. With days left in our trip, I suddenly wished I'd made a longer list so I had more things to look forward to.

Reindeer out of sight, we boarded the bus. The wind had sapped warmth from my legs, and I was just getting it back when we reached Dettifoss.

Dettifoss is the most powerful waterfall in Europe. 17,657 cubic ft of water fall every second during high season,[2] a wave of white, frothy water that's not dissimilar to Niagara Falls. 148 ft tall, 328 ft wide, it's hard to capture the entire feature in a photograph. A trail along

---

2. Visit North Iceland. *Dettifoss Waterfall.* 2023 https://www.northiceland.is/en/place/dettifoss-waterfall

the cliff edge provided a good view, looking up the river at it, but the canyon was too narrow and the froth too large to see the entire height of the waterfall. It's impossible to escape the roar.

While the churn of the falls turned the water white, it did have a slightly milky look downriver. This is the result of glacier flour, sediment carried from Vatnajökull.[3] And if that name sounds familiar, it's the giant ice cap that gave name to Iceland's largest national park, the one in which we had a glacier hike. Here we were, two days later and on a different part of the island, still exploring everything the park had to offer.

Like Niagara, you can see Dettifoss from either side of the river. That's another item to do on a potential third trip, see it from the west side. A benefit of seeing it from the west is the ability to catch a glimpse of Selfoss upriver. It's also from that side Dettifoss might look familiar, as it's featured in a scene in the 2012 movie Prometheus.[4]

Dettifoss loosely translates to 'collapsing waterfall' based on how the water tumbles,[5] but its little sister upstream, Selfoss, translates to 'seal waterfall'[6]. Short but long, it doesn't have the same power. Instead, it's a series of small falls in a shepherd's hook pattern, with

---

3. World of Waterfalls. *Dettifoss.* 2021 https://www.world-of-waterfalls.com/waterfalls/iceland-dettifoss/

4. Wikipedia. *Dettifoss.* 2022 https://en.wikipedia.org/wiki/Dettifoss

5. Adventures. *Dettifss Waterfall: The Most Powerful Waterfall in Europe.* 2023 https://adventures.com/iceland/attractions/waterfalls/dettifoss-waterfall/

6. WordSense. *Selfoss.* 2023 https://www.wordsense.eu/Selfoss/

the hook furthest upriver. The flow has increased recently, a climate change concern that could mean Selfoss and Dettifoss will erode the cliffs they fall from, moving further and further upriver.[7]

Time constraints meant I couldn't get close to Selfoss, but I was desperate to see it. The likelihood of ever seeing this waterfall again was lower than my chance to see another aurora. Vikki and I convinced Mom and Michele to head to the bus while we jogged the side trail. We ran into Nathan and the woman the Australians thought he was crushing on. Vikki kept sneaking glances at them, but I concentrated on finding a spot to take a quick photo. We had twenty minutes before the bus was scheduled to leave.

Photos were quick snapshots before we powerwalked to the parking lot. I was happy it wouldn't *just* be Vikki and I the group waited for. We made good time, the four of us making a point to not dally. We arrived as a few other people finished a bathroom break, and all guilt, small as it was, for seeing Selfoss disappeared.

Dettifoss is part of the Diamond Circle. A companion to Reykjavik's Golden Circle, the Diamond Circle is comprised of four locations in north Iceland: Lake Mývatn, Dettifoss Waterfall, Ásbyrgi Canyon, and the fishing town of Húsavík.[8]

Dettifos was the only location we saw up close, but I spied Lake Mývatn a few times. I would love to see Ásbyrgi in the future. It's

---

7. World of Waterfalls. *Selfoss.* 2021 https://www.world-of-waterfalls.com/waterfalls/iceland-selfoss/

8. Guide to Iceland. *The Ultimate Guide to Iceland's Diamond Circle.* Michael Chapman. 2023 https://guidetoiceland.is/best-of-iceland/the-ultimate-guide-to-the-diamond-circle

Iceland's version of the Grand Canyon, by which I mean it's large, but what's at the bottom is not a gushing river like the Colorado but instead a rare (for Iceland) forest. [9]

Can you imagine, a winding river of trees in the crack of the earth? Even if all I get to do is stand at the rim of Ásbyrgi, it's on my bucket list.

---

9. Guide to Iceland. *Ásbyrgi Travel Guide.* 2023 https://guidetoiceland.is/travel-iceland/drive/asbyrgi

Námaskarð & NASA

The Námaskarð geothermal area is a small collection of features that is easy to see out your window and a location I imagine most road-trippers would skip. I wouldn't blame them, unlike the hot springs in Geysir, these smelled strongly of sulfur. With the wind still strong, we only noticed the smell up close thankfully. In some places, the steam from cone-shaped chimneys was completely horizontal, giving us walk-through, smelly steam treatments.

Aside from the pools of bubbling water, there wasn't much to the surrounding landscape. Colorful, but dull at the same time because nothing was bright. Just there. When I first saw it through the bus window, my mind went *Mars*. I assumed the area might have been the setting of a science fiction movie I hadn't realized was filmed on the island.

I'm not the only one who thought it looked like Mars – NASA did too.

NASA has come to Iceland several times. The first was 1965[1] when NASA brought the Apollo astronauts to train them as geologists. Everyone selected to be on the space shuttle were pilots, so to conduct the experiments NASA wanted they needed some on-the-ground training.

In the Sixties, there was speculation that astronauts would encounter moon rocks formed from the movement of tectonic plates and volcanic flows. Iceland is full of such rocks, and so was the ideal place to teach how to identify them. Harrison Schmitt, who was part of the Apollo 17 mission, mentioned picking through glacial outwashes in particular had been useful. The variety of rocks clustered together resembled the complexities of lunar surface debris he came across.

Out of all the locations visited for Apollo training – the Grand Canyon, Hawai'i, Alaska, Meteor Crater in Arizona – astronauts said Iceland was the closest to the moon.

NASA visited Askja, 44 miles from the Námaskarð geothermal area, twice. First in 1965, and again in 1967. Askja is another UNESCO World Heritage Site part of Vatnajökull National Park[2] but it's pretty bleak. Lots of gravel, no vegetation. Parts of the region haven't been named, but one of the canyons is called Nautagil, taking 'naut' from astronaut, even as the word means "bull" in Icelandic.

---

1. The Exploration Museum. *Apollo Astronaut Training in Iceland.* 2023 https://www.explorationmuseum.com/astronaut-training/

2. Iceland Air. *In the Footsetps of the Apollo Astronauts.* Egill Bjarnason. 2021 https://www.icelandair.com/blog/in-the-footsteps-of-the-apollo-astronauts/

Names aren't the only legacy the Apollo program left behind – there's an exhibit at the Exploration Museum in Húsavík.[3]

When Apollo 11 brought back Moon rocks, it was determined Iceland's geography may *look* like the moon, but the geology was different. So different that NASA didn't return to the Icelandic highlands for decades until it came time to train for Mars.

Mars has similar landscape features, even if the rocks are different, which made Iceland a good training ground for rovers and drones. A 2019 trip allowed for a test of robot capability and served as practice for the humans guiding them. One trial focused on rover control and drone pairing – sending out helicopters to scope the landscape before determining where to guide the rover.[4] Another was using new 3D technology to map a lava tube, a geographic feature of Iceland and Mars.[5]

I'm still kicking myself for not knowing about the Apollo missions to Iceland prior to this trip. I wouldn't call myself a space nut, but I've taken a few astronomy classes and once upon a time, I thought it would be neat to study black holes. One of my career brags is having

---

3. The Times. *Askja, Iceland – Visit the Place Where Astronauts Trained For The Moon Landing.* Will Hide. July 20th, 2019 https://www.thetimes.co.uk/article/askja-iceland-visit-the-place-where-the-moon-landing-astronauts-trained-ssq8ds5ks

4. Nasa. *NASA Tests Mars Systems in Iceland.* Noah Michelsohn. Oct 29, 2019 https://www.nasa.gov/feature/nasa-tests-mars-systems-in-iceland/

5. SpaceRef. *Drone Maps Icy Lava Tube in Iceland in Preparation for Cave Exploration on the Moon and Mars.* Marc Boucher. March 19th, 2019 https://spaceref.com/science-and-exploration/drone-maps-icy-lava-tube-in-iceland-in-preparation-for-cave-exploration-on-the-moon-and-mars/

a first-round interview with NASA – not for anything sciencey but rather to help with their social media. My career aspirations pivoted as I got older, but sometimes I still think those jobs I imagined in middle school and high school were cool.

Black hole researcher.

Zoo exhibit designer.

Horse trainer.

Librarian.

Eh, part-time author is close enough.

Mývatn Baths

From the Námaskarð geothermal area we headed to the Mývatn baths. They're not as famous as the Blue Lagoon and the water lacks the silica responsible for its unique coloring, but the Mývatn baths are still filled with mineral-rich geothermal water. Particularly, it's rich in sulfur which is considered good for respiratory issues like asthma.[1] You can't smell the sulfur, thankfully, and the pools are smaller than we explored at Blue Lagoon. It's also shallower,[2] which made Vikki happy.

Location and size mean the Mývatn baths are less touristy, which makes them charming in my opinion. The spa sits on a hillside, the main pool hosting a rock wall and bar while the second extends to the edge of the carved-out plateau. It's not quite an invisible horizon,

---

1. Mývatn Nature Baths. *Lagoon.* 2023 https://myvatnnaturebaths.is/lagoon

2. Laidback Trip. *A Complete Guide to Myvatn Nature Baths.* Lucie Hermankova and Martin Tychtl. Feb 2nd, 2023 https://www.laidbacktrip.com/posts/myvatn-nature-baths-travel-guide

but you could swim out and look down onto Lake Mývatn nestled in the valley below.

I attempted to take in the view, but the second pool was completely exposed. The wind hadn't let up, and it was strong enough to cause problems opening and shutting doors. It stripped the warmth from the second pool, keeping guests in the main pool, partially sheltered by the buildings.

Weather aside, the spa was nice. We sat low in the water, eager to get out of the wind. The swim-in bar had a good selection and a tall decorative rock feature worked as a windbreak. We chatted in the warm, blue water, enjoying the heat seeping into our legs. After days of hiking, it felt good, and the strong wind barely impacted our ability to enjoy the water in the main pool.

There were two things the Mývatn baths had Blue Lagoon didn't, which I wish I had gotten the chance to appreciate. The first was a separate hot tub roughly twenty degrees warmer than the pool.[3] With the wind chill, I would have loved the extra warmth, but it was small and thus too crowded for me. The other was a deck area. There's not much out-of-water lounge space at Blue Lagoon, but there was a section at Mývatn. On a sunnier day, I would have loved to sit there with a book, dipping in and out of the water like I would at a beach.

Getting ready for lunch was an unexpected toss back to undergrad. Blue Lagoon had plenty of private showers and changing rooms, but Mývatn only had two private showers for the entire locker room. I

---

3. Guide to Iceland. *Myvatn Nature Baths Travel Guide.* 2023 https://guidetoiceland.is/travel-iceland/drive/myvatn-nature-baths

couldn't bring myself to shower and lather naked as I had in the gym during my college years; I sudsed up in my swimsuit in the communal showers.

Several women followed my lead, also looking uncertain. Sometimes I wish America accepted casual nudity because I think its lack is tied to many self-esteem issues the beauty industry caters to (and encourages). We're always presented with idealized versions of bodies in movies and ads, and now with AI Tiktok filters we're doing the same thing to ourselves.

Just like transparency is important, I think authenticity is too. It can widen the understanding of what's normal. Maybe seeing the bodies of people of all ages would change that, making us less body shy, less willing to change ourselves, less likely to think we're wrong. Maybe I wouldn't have hated my curls when they first came in, the only girl in 5th grade with them. Maybe it wouldn't be so hard to find shoes that fit my feet if the industry knew how common my issues were.

I recently chatted with friends about how our thirties were better than our twenties. Not only because we had more money, but because we'd shaken off a few of society's expectations and ideas of normal. It's okay for me to buy guy sandals, to forgo lipstick.

And it's okay for me to be in my early thirties, traveling abroad as a single ace woman. It's okay for me to not want the relationship my parents or some friends have. It's okay for me to not want children.

In hindsight, I wish I had the confidence to have stripped in that commercial shower at the Mývatn. Maybe that's something I'll learn in my forties.

Dark Castles

Our post-lunch attraction was a walk through a small, sheltered forest – a rarity for Iceland. Early settlers cut down so many trees that the impact is still felt, but there has been a concentrated effort to build up national woods. Most of the trees around Reykjavik are transports, non-native species brought to fill small green squares, but in the east and north highlands, there are a few forests to explore.

I'm using the word forest loosely. I grew up down the street from 50 acres of woods I'd get lost in as a middle schooler. I've hiked the redwoods. I've been on deer paths so narrow and green you can't see the trunks of trees ten feet away. Compared to that, the forest of Dimmuborgir is small and thin. I don't think there was a single tree over seven feet tall, and I could have walked between them in shorts, unworried about scrapes from undergrowth.

That said, it is still a lovely area filled with small silver birch trees. In the depts of September, each was heavy with golden leaves. Scattered through them were small, red bushes. Because this forest grows in the middle of an old lava field, the bursts of autumn colors stood out against the black and brown rock. The field had tall pillars, lopsided mounds, and small caves capable of holding several people. It's how Dimmuborgir got its name - 'Dark Castles'.[1] Some of the pillars certainly looked like wicked castle spires, but I'd never want to feast in any of the cave halls.

2,300 years ago, lava flowed into the lake that existed where Dimmuborgir sits. As the water and wet terrain boiled, hot steam burst through the lava and the chutes they created were immortalized as pillars. The geological effect can be seen elsewhere in Iceland, but usually, the pillars are tiny hills that look like rocky moguls, not these features that are twenty or thirty feet high. The only other place in the world where similar pillars exist is at the bottom of the ocean off the coast of Mexico. They're a rare treat to explore.

The unique nature of the place, and its dark rock, have led to interesting myths. In Norwegian folklore, Dimmuborgir is where Satan fell when he was cast out of heaven and his digging into the earth formed the caves. Icelandic folklore also connects the darkness of lava tubes to unfriendly creatures, usually trolls. Dimmuborgir is considered the home of the Icelandic Yule Lads.[2]

All thirteen of them are the sons of the half-troll, half-ogre Grýla and her husband Leppalúði. Grýla has a taste for children, and her favorite ones to eat are those who didn't get clothes for Christmas. While the origins are thought to be an old warning to encourage

---

1. Arctic Adventures. *Dimmuborgir: The Incredible Lava Field Near Lake Myvatn in North Iceland.* 2023 https://adventures.is/iceland/attractions/dimmuborgir/

2. Guide to Iceland. *Dimmuborgir Travel Guide.* 2023 https://guidetoiceland.is/travel-iceland/drive/dimmuborgir

children to finish their weaving/knitting/sewing projects for winter sets in, it's a belief that still lingers in modern Iceland. Our tour guide, married and with a kid due in the next month, admitted he still gets socks every Christmas from his mother to ward off a hungry Grýla.

Grýla's sons come out the thirteen nights before Christmas, starting December 12th, to terrorize the people of Iceland, with each lad acting according to his name.[3] Sheep-Colt Clod terrifies livestock, Window-Peeper looks into homes to find things to steal. They've been pacified over the years, transforming from monsters meant to discourage outdoor travel during the coldest Icelandic winter nights to trolls that will gobble up your skyr (Icelandic yogurt) and leave presents in exchange.

In modern mythology, Dimmuborgir was a Game of Thrones filming location. More specifically, where Mance Rayder's wildling army camped.

The park is full of crisscrossing paved trails; it was the only place on this trip where our guide actively led us instead of simply pointing out the trailhead. He was worried we would take a wrong turn and get lost among the trees and pillars. Even if I hadn't gotten lost, I don't think I would have been for long. There was lots of signage, and even if I couldn't understand it I would have been able to recognize repeats.

---

3. Smithsonian Mag. *Meet the Thirteen Yule Lads, Iceland's Own Mischievous Santa Clauses.* Rachel Nuwer. Dec 17th, 2013 https://www.smithsonianmag.com/smart-news/meet-the-thirteen-yule-lads-icelands-own-mischievous-santa-clauses-180948162/

Eventually, we were led out of the forest, climbing up a hill to watch the clouds drift away as the wind slowly died. By the time we got to our next destination, the weather was near perfect.

Waterfall of the Gods

As a child, I remember visiting the Grand Canyon and being so overwhelmed by the size it didn't feel 3D. Goðafoss didn't have the same effect on me, but close.

Goðafoss got its name from a mix of history and myth, thanks to the actions of Thorgeir Ljosvetningagodi in 1000 AD.[1] At the time, Iceland was under the control of Norway and its king, Olav Tryggvason.[2] He's often known as Olav I. A huge supporter of Christianity, the king pressured Iceland to officially convert and become a Christian nation. While there was a Christian population on the island,[3] many Islanders held onto the traditional beliefs of

---

1. Wikipedia. *Thorgeir Ljosvetningagodi*. 2021 https://en.wikipedia.org/wiki/Thorgeir_Ljosvetningagodi

2. Wikipedia. *Olaf Tryggvason*. 2023 https://en.wikipedia.org/wiki/Olaf_Tryggvason

3. Wikipedia. *Religion in Iceland*. 2023. https://en.wikipedia.org/wiki/Religion_in_Iceland

Norse Paganism.[4] The debate in Iceland's government was fierce, with support for paganism strong enough there was a chance the country would go to war against Norway for religious freedom.[5]

The conflict worried Ljosvetningagodi. He had the influence to sway a large part of the Icelandic parliament, AlÞing, in either direction and knew he needed to make the right choice. After meditating on the issue, he decided to convince the populace to convert to Christianity.[6] He threw his support behind the religion, renouncing his traditional beliefs, and symbolically tossed his Nordic idols over a waterfall - Goðafoss.[7] Today, his choice is considered a brave action that preemptively stopped a war and saved the lives of countless people.

Goðafoss is not the tallest, most powerful, or even widest waterfall we saw, but there's a majesty to it I love. Standing on the rocks lining its pool, you have to turn your head to see the whole span of the falls. It's a wide horseshow, with two juts of rock separating the streams as the water turns from flat grey to frothy white lace before reaching into a deep, wide pool. The roar was great, but not overwhelming, and I found myself simply enjoying the sound and shape of the water

---

4. Conversion Among the Germanic Peoples. Carole M. Cusack. 1998

5. Speculum. *Late and Peaceful: Iceland's Conversion Through Arbitration in 1000.* Jenny Jochens. 1999

6. Saga Museum. *17 Exhibits From the Icelandic Sagas.* 2017 https://www.sagamuseum.is/overview/#thorgeir-ljosvetningagodi

7. Glacial Experience. *The Historic Goðafoss Waterfall in North-Iceland – the Waterfall of the Gods.* Regína Hrönn Ragnarsdóttir. 2023 https://glacialexperience.is/the-historical-godafoss-waterfall-in-north-iceland-the-waterfall-of-the-gods/

going over the falls. If the ground wasn't so pointy, I could have easily meditated.

"Time to go!" our guide said, shepherding us back to the bus. I dragged my feet, looking down at the river snaking away from Goðafoss. There was so much daylight left in the day, couldn't we stay? I could see another path that ambled downriver past the bus.

"Let's go, Gin!" Mom and Michele said, powerwalking past me.

With a sigh, I made my way to the bus.

The drive to the hotel was notable for one reason – mountain tunnels.

Despite being a necessity when winter conditions make the ring road impassable, Iceland's tunnels are recent constructions. Twelve of the country's fourteen tunnels were built after 1991.[8] Before that, if the road was closed due to snow, ice, or other extreme weather, there was no option but to turn back. We traveled through one of the longest tunnels in the country, almost five miles of darkness in a two-lane tunnel. When we exited, the sudden daylight hurt my eyes.

As we drove to Akureyri, our guide gave us bad news. There was a storm on the horizon, and the whale-watching tour the next morning was canceled because the sea would be too dangerous. Instead, we'd have a more relaxed morning and not leave the hotel till 10 am. Michele and Mom were excited at the prospect of sleeping in, but I probably wouldn't. I like to keep habits if I can – even working from home due to COVID I kept my 7 am alarm.

---

8. Wikipedia. *List of tunnels in Iceland.* 2022 https://en.wikipedia.org/wiki/List_of_tunnels_in_Iceland

Akureyri is considered the capital of the North. With a population of 17,000, it's the largest city in the region and houses a university. It sits at the edge of a fjord, sheltered from the ocean but not immune to rough water. The bridge we crossed to get there looked less like a bridge and more like asphalt that floated on half a mile of water. Flat, minimal railing. I can see why our guide pushed us to leave Goðafoss – I too would want sunlight to see it.

Since we got to town before dinner, we dumped our stuff in our hotel rooms and walked downtown. Mom hoped to shop, but most of the stores were closed. They tend to close early in Iceland, which was low-key frustrating to her. I sorta understand it. I'm used to strolling a street before or after dinner, looking at the items in one boutique or another, but that's hard to do in Iceland when most stores close at 6pm. Their open hours made shopping hard around a tourist schedule, were we sometimes didn't finish a day's activities until 6 or 7. We would have needed to arrive in Akureyri at least two hours earlier to allow Mom to shop like she wanted, giving up at least one attraction, and personally, I'd much rather take in the natural beauty of Iceland than the stocks on its shelves.

We window-shopped stores and restaurants, eyeing menus. A pizzeria place caught our eyes, which meant we *didn't* order pizza. Compared to many Reykjavik restaurants, this was open and felt modern. Dinner conversation flipped to what we'd like so far, showing off photos we hadn't shared yet, and Michele commented on the attractiveness of some of the people around us. After a few nudges, I pulled out my phone to update my Hinge location.

"Find us some hot Icelandic men," Michele asked.

Alas, there were only three people in Akureyri and two were women. I understand swiping through people an djust looking can simply be a fun game, but it's never a game I'll be able to honestly play. Even my first celebrity crush was one I selected because I like the character, versus any aesthetic attraction.

As we walked back to the hotel, uphill in the dark, we could feel the storm our guide mentioned closing in. The wind picked up and my cheeks developed a sting I associate with freezing temperatures. I hoped things didn't get too bad; I hadn't packed any winter gear. I could always layer, maybe double up on my neck warmers, but the next day might be very, very brutal.

Akureyri Storms

Vikki and I woke at our normal time, giving ourselves the luxury of long showers. At breakfast, we were informed of yet another delay in leaving as our guide stayed up to date on the storm. Akureyri hadn't seen bad weather, but the areas we would be traveling through had been hit.

To kill time, Vikki and I played cards in the hotel lobby. We didn't have a table in our room, but sitting near the front doors meant we frequently got hit with bursts of cold air.

At one point, I put down my hand to stare out the automatic doors. "Vikki, it's snowing!"

We hoped the storm wouldn't hit the city, but alas, it looked like it might soon be time to add on a third layer. As I dealt another hand, the Australian women hurried outside without coats. They held out their hands to catch the flakes, smiling as they looked up. It was the first time one of them had even *seen* snow.

The snow didn't stick, but the cold remained. Still tracking the weather, our guide pushed our departure way back, to 2 pm, and gave us alternative activities for the day. The local lagoon on the company's dime or spend the day in town.

Vikki and I looked at each other. We'd seen a bookstore with a coffee shop last night, and the idea of sitting there reading a book for the morning and early afternoon sounded delightful. *Town!* we voted in the chat, and Mom and Michele said the same.

We weren't the only people who enjoyed the idea of a bookstore day. While some people stayed at the hotel, a few joined us at the bookstore. We settled in with coffee and books – mine from the States, while others bought local reads.

Mom, Michele, and another older solo traveler visited the nearby church and then got in a bit of shopping. They joined us about noon, Michele with a bag of books for her grandchildren, and Mom with a glass of wine to enjoy while reading.

My whole family are readers. During summer breaks, I had to read for thirty minutes before I could turn on the TV. It wasn't much of a hardship, and sharing book recs is a family hobby, as is reading by the fireplace in winter.

I'd brought a romance, which ended up being steamier than I expected. I'm glad no one walked behind me to check out the magazines, but I certainly shifted my position every so often to hide the words from Alec, Nathan's cousin, beside me. I didn't want him to think I normally read such things, and I certainly didn't want knowledge of what I was reading to make its way to his cousin's ear. He and Nathan didn't seem to have that type of relationship, and I still wasn't sure if Nathan was crushing on me, but I still found myself shifting constantly to shield my pages.

Though I had promised myself to not return with more books than I brought, the lure of a bookstore was too much and I bought two. A book on Icelandic folktales and a historical fiction called The Sealwoman's Gift based on the Turkish Abductions.

In the 1600s, there were pirate slave raids along the coast of Iceland. Nearly 400 Icelanders were captured and sold into slavery in African markets. Only 50 of them got their freedom back.[1] It plays a significant role in Icelandic history, not only because of the numerous firsthand accounts that have survived but also because it's the only military attack on Iceland that resulted in a loss of life.[2]

Returning to our table with my purchases, the power in the bookstore went out. There was enough grey daylight coming in from the wide windows we could read, but with no power, so too went the POS system. We couldn't buy anything from books to wine to tea, but thankfully the shop stayed open and no one was shuffled out.

I didn't know it at the time, but half the country had gone dark.[3] The worst part of the country hit had been the roads we'd traveled through the previous day, with reports of wind gusts at hurricane speeds. Later, our guide showed us photos his father had taken in Djúpivogur, cars shoved together with the windows blown out. The force of the wind had been enough to obliterate them, leaving chunks of glass on the seats and surrounding ground. Tourists traveling on

---

1. Wikipedia. *Turkish Abductions*. 2023 https://en.wikipedia.org/wiki/Turkish_Abductions

2. Your Friend In Reykjavik. *Pirate Attack in Iceland – The Turkish Abductions*. Feb 3rd, 2023. https://yourfriendinreykjavik.com/pirate-attack-in-iceland-the-turkish-abductions/

the road had to be evacuated, [4] but the Artic Adventures group behind us had never left the hotel so they were all safe.

Where we were in Akureyri was relatively calm in comparison, but the city did have serious flooding outside the downtown area. [5] Those who went to the lagoon reported the road nearly being washed out by waves. The only reason the bus hadn't turned around was no place to do so.

When the power returned to downtown, our bookstore troop headed across the street to a French café for a late lunch before our pick-up. The place was filled with warm wood and well lit pastry displays none of use could resist. We were the last on board and took what seats remained.

The weather delay meant that for us to make it to our next hotel before dark, we couldn't stop for a small hike like we had originally planned. It was probably for the best. While the rains that had hit the area early had faded, fog laid thick on the road as we traveled west along the north coast. I could only start to see the fields on either side of the road.

The bus took on a quiet tone, moving up and down hills we couldn't properly see through a landscape we could only imagine. Usually, our tour guide had something to say – some personal tale or historical knowledge – but he was silent.

---

4. High North News. *East Iceland Battered By Storms*. Trine Jonassen. Jan 2nd, 2023 https://www.highnorthnews.com/en/east-iceland-battered-storms

5. Visir. *The First Autumn Depression Hit the Country With Force*. Hallgerður Kolbrún E. Jónsdóttir. Sept 25, 2022 https://www.visir.is/g/20222315966d via Google Translate

I think he white-knuckled that leg. If we'd left three hours prior, we might have been another collection of tourists to rescue.

Troll Peninsula

We stopped at a gas station after two and a half hours of driving. Normally such time is nothing – I will drive the five hours between Chicago and Detroit several times a year – but that was the longest continuous time we'd ever spent on the bus.

Everyone tumbled out, excited to stretch our legs and peer through the slowly fading fog. It felt so weird, having sat for most of the day. First the bookstore café, then the bus. We'd all gotten used to multiple small hikes a day.

I walked around the gas station, stretching my legs. I'd become a fan of a local candy, Prince Polo, and was happy to find a variety of flavors to try. I filled my hands, already debating if taste tasting was a good bus activity or if I should simply continue making progress in my podcast queue. I got distracted by Vikki's attempts to care for a stray cat near the pumps, who traded a hot dog for scritches and allowed Vikki to pick her up. "She just needs some love," Vikki said, offering the cat's head to anyone who wanted a pet.

It wasn't a sheep, but at least she got an animal photo!

As soon as Vikki got back on the bus, Michele poured hand sanitizer into her palm.

After the gas station, we continued our dive. The lifting fog allowed us to view Tröllaskagi, the Troll Peninsula. It takes roughly three hours to circle the peninsula,[1] which juts into the cold waters of the Greenland Sea. It's considered one of the more scenic drives of the country, with large peaks on one side and the ocean on the other. The road cuts close to the water in places, and that morning it had been covered in water so I'm glad we waited in Akureyri, even if it meant we didn't have the time to stop at a scenic overlook. While we had visibility, the cloud cover was thick enough that it felt like 4 pm during February for most of the drive. It's an area I'd love to hike in better weather.

Our guide filled the time by telling us about Icelandic trolls. My dad's side of the family has Norwegian blood, and my grandfather had a fondness for their trolls. Short creatures with ugly faces, there were always a few of them around the house and garden. Icelandic trolls by contrast are giants with a fondness for darkness – living in caves, lava tubes, and nocturnal. If hit by sunlight, the large creatures would be turned to stone and could be mistaken for boulders or mountains.

They're common antagonists of Icelandic fables, like the Yule Lads that live in Dimmuborgir.

Our guide's favorite story was about a boy named Jon and his cow.[2]

---

1. Laidback Trip. *A Guide to Trollaskagi Peninsula in Iceland*. Lucie Hermankova and Martin Tychtl. Feb, 2023 https://www.laidbacktrip.com/posts/trollaskagi-peninsula-travel-guide

When the cow, Búkolla goes missing, Jon's parents tell him to find her and not return until he does. He travels over the land, calling out to the cow and following the sound of her moos. He finds her tied in a cave, where an ogress and her daughter plan to slaughter and eat Búkolla. Jon unties the cow and starts to lead her home. However, they are spotted by the ogress and her daughter. They give chase and gain ground quickly. Jon turns to Búkolla and asks what should he do?

Búkolla says to pluck a hair from her tail and toss it on the ground. As Jon does, Búkolla casts a spell, commanding the hair to become a stream so wide only a bird could cross. Seeing this, the ogress calls out to her daughter and tells her to grab the family bull. The bull, which is enormous, drinks the entire stream.

Jon asks Búkolla again what they should do and the cow tells him to pluck another hair from her tail and toss it on the ground. This time, Búkolla chants a spell that turns the hair into a line of fire so hot only a bird can cross. When the ogress sees this, she again instructs her daughter to bring over the bull. It proceeds to pee on the fire, dowsing the flames.

With the ogress closing in fast, Jon turns to Búkolla for aid for a third time. This time, the cow turns her hair into a tall mountain that only a bird can cross. Frustrated, the ogress yells at Jon and tells her daughter to get her father's drill.

The ogress starts drilling, eager to get at Jon because he's annoying and at Búkolla to eat her. However, she becomes overzealous. As soon as the hole is big enough to see through, she attempts to squeeze herself into it like a tunnel. She becomes stuck, her rear sticking out of the mountain, and turns to stone when dawn breaks.

"And there's her butt," our guide said, pointing to a lumpy backside of a mountain that comes into view after a turn. We laughed, and he directed our attention to an island off the coast.

Tall, wide, and flat, our guide told us it used to be a troll cow. A troll couple had attempted to lead it across the fjord in search of a bull, but they lost track of time. When dawn broke, all three of them turned to stone out in the water.[3] The husband troll is gone now, eroded to time, but the wife is still a narrow, weathered pillar before the flat island.

By the end of the day, the weather calmed so we explored a small river gorge. Compared to others we'd seen this trip, it wasn't impressive, but it was so good to get off the bus and take a breath of air. The smell of rain lingered on the grasses around us, but we were inland enough the ground wasn't a muddy squelch. This part of the island had gotten wet, but not flooded.

Vikki ignored the water tumbling under a bridge for the sheep pastures across it. Her sheep selfie the morning after we had first seen the aurora wasn't as close as she'd hoped, and with the tour almost over she couldn't give up an opportunity to get a better one. I walked with her toward the pasture, but there was no indication of a roaming path. No ladder to go over the fence, no gate, and the sheep we could see were so far off Vikki could cover two with a fist.

"I really wanted a sheep photo, Ginny," she pouted as we walked back to the bus.

"We have one day left, including a farm visit. There's still hope."

---

3. Gray Line. *4 Stories of Trolls Who Turned into Rocks.* July 19th, 2021 https://grayline.is/blog/4-stories-of-trolls-who-turned-into-rocks

"Not the same. I wanted one because it reminded me of the sheep in Mongolia. They don't have farms there, it's all open grazing."

I linked my arms with hers. "Maybe there's be sheep at this hotel too?"

While our next place indeed sat isolated with a perfect hill grazing behind it there were no sheep. We enjoyed our last bottle of wine from Reykjavik in Mom and Michele's room. While not our last night in Iceland, it was our last on the tour which left a bitter-sweet taste in our mouths. We were having fun, we didn't want to go back, and oddly enough, kept talking about how we'd miss the beds.

We'd been sharing doubles all trip, but Icelandic doubles are European doubles, which means it's not one giant mattress, but twins placed next to each other. And with two mattresses came two sets of bedclothes. Vikki and I might have shared a headboard and footboard, but we'd been granted our own sheets and comforters every night. Each had been warm and comfortable, and there had been no complaints from anyone about stolen covers. Vikki and Michele both took photos of the tags on the duvets for future reference.

Dinner was a large, fun affair as we talked about the highlights of the trip with all our bus mates. We'd be on the bus together the next day, but after our last day of activities, we'd be dropped off at different hotels. I ended up chatting about my job to some of the older couples.

It's always interesting explaining marketing tech to an older generation compared to fellow Millennials. We all know that we're being tracked, and why, but it's usually such a shock to Boomers and above. To be fair, I'm not sure most people my age realize *how much* data is shared, aggregated, and bought for the sake of advertising targeting.

And sometimes, not even advertising. For social listening projects, the entire web is scraped.

I remember my first time doing such a project for a pharmaceutical company and realizing the tools I worked with were reading and categorizing medical forums. Struggles with depression or conceiving weren't just shared with a private online community. I was reading those too, looking for insights. Sometimes the answers I hunted down were benign things, like what's a fall flavor people like other than pumpkin or how the public feels about a brand. Other times, it was trying to understand pain points like confusion about how to use a service or the impact a condition had on someone's life so a solution could be presented in an ad.

Of course, I regularly work with a company that tracks what stores you go to as well. Saw a TV ad, then went into that retailer? I know it. And I know if that ad made you go in one extra time a month. In aggregate, of course.

It can, I'll admit, be creepy. I employ doublethink a bit in my everyday life.

With the conclusion of dinner, and still a good deal of wine left, several women gathered in the lobby to drink and talk. Mom glowed, she loves talking to people and sharing advice, and the conversation turned to the struggles of being a career woman. Michele would have had a lot to share too, but she'd elected to take a nap prior to looking for the aurora.

The red wine lured me to sleep, and Vikki couldn't convince me to go out and look at the skies later.

"Come on, Ginny," she cajoled. "It's our last night! Our last chance to see it!"

The forecast had been weak, and the night was bitter cold. I wouldn't say my appetite for the Northern Lights was gone, but now that I had fifty images of it on my phone, the steps I needed to get ten more transformed from speed bumps to two-foot hurdles.

"Have fun," I told her, and she huffed out to join Michele.

I was asleep before Vikki returned. She told me the next morning it hadn't been very impressive, the weakest showing all trip. I sipped my coffee, relieved and feeling haughty at my decision to stay cozy.

Triplet Craters

We left the hotel, happy the weather was loads better than the previous day, to do a small hike near triplet craters called Grábrókargígar, though the smallest is nearly impossible to see anymore.[1] They'd formed in a way I never heard of, not by a volcano blowing their top off, or a meteor strike, but a slow buildup of a rim by flowing lava from the center.

The day was windy, but not annoyingly so, and after getting a good view of the center of the largest crater, Stóra Grábrók, I trotted up the stairs to walk the rim. After being sedimentary yesterday, it felt good to move. I took giant steps to a lookout.

The day was clear; I could see for miles. Small mountains, or volcanos because you can never be too sure in Iceland, were on either side of the road and everything was covered in a muted green. The brown of fall would come eventually, but there was too little sun and

---

1. Outdoor Project. *Grábrókargígar National Monument.* Nick Catania. 2023 https://www.outdoorproject.com/iceland/grabrokargigar-natural-monument

too much rain for the color to have left the landscape entirely. I stood staring, breathing in the air, taking in what might be my last, good view of the Icelandic highlands.

I felt sad. I wasn't ready to go, even as I felt the needs and pressure of work start to creep in. Had my team done well without me? How many emails were sitting in my inbox right that very minute? I'd already helped with one issue, asynchronously over two days. Were there more things I'd need to jump in on?

Michele joined me. "I'm going to miss this," she said, staring at the view.

"Yeah," I admitted. "Me too."

I chatted with Nathan again, walking around the rim, and this time when I passed Vikki I didn't get any sly looks. Whether she believed the Australians that his interest lay with someone else, knew I wasn't interested, or figured these last eight hours of a group wasn't enough time for anything, I couldn't guess. I know shipping culture is rampant in fandom spaces, which I'll admit I hang out in a lot, but having that culture turned on you, having someone imagine you in a relationship with a third person, I'm hoping bothers allos as much as aces and aros.

It's something I've always lived with, but I truly, *truly* enjoy interactions where such thoughts and emotions are absent.

Off the side of the mountain were old sheep pens, and I was surprised at how small they were. Icelandic sheep are given free rein for the spring and summer. Come September, they're rounded up in an event called réttir, which is considered such a wonder it has its own Atlas Obscura entry.[2]

There are roughly 800,000 sheep in Iceland, a little more than double the country's population of 347,000.[3] Once rounded up, usually on foot and horseback, the sheep are led into a large paddock and the farmers start sorting by identifying their sheep and putting them in a small pen adjacent to the main one. These pen systems frequently look like sliced pizzas, with a round centerpiece, but we'd also seen a rectangular layout with the group pen in the center and individual farmers' pens on the left and right.

For all the pens we saw out the window, we never saw one in use. I stared at the pens of the Old Brekka Corral, wondering how many sheep could fit into a farmer's pen. Surly no more than twenty, maybe forty if they were smooshed. Was forty a big flock in 1964, the last year that moss-covered string of pens had been in use? It's not like the corral had been retired for being too small – it had been damaged in a flood according to the plaque.[4] It seemed as good a reason as any to the locals to build a new one in a different spot.

Like Icelandic Horses, Icelandic Sheep are an isolated and thus pure breed, leading to a lot of traditional pride around both animals. Sheep tourism is new but is starting to become an event hotels and

---

2. Atlas Obscura. *Rettir*. Kerry Wolfe. 2023 https://www.atlasobscura.com/foods/rettir-iceland-sheep

3. WorldoMeter. *Iceland Population*. 2023 https://www.worldometers.info/world-population/iceland-population/

4. Minjastofnun Island *Interesting stuff*. *Gamla-Brekkrott*. 2023 https://www.minjastofnun.is/is/ahugavert

tour groups are offering packages for. I have no desire to go out of my way to attend a réttir, but I can understand the want to watch. Seeing the Pony Round up on Chincoteague Island[5] has been something I've always wanted to do, inspired by my love of horses and found memory of the book *Misty of Chincoteague* I read as a child.

Réttir happens every September, but with each local region hosting its own there's no national date to plan a trip around. Rounding up the sheep can take up to a week, but sorting is usually done in a day followed by dancing, feasting, and drinking.[6]

Once rounded up, sheep are shaved or butchered. Lamp consumption is on the decline in the country, but it remains part of traditional cuisine just like the traditional Iceland sweater. Not, I'll admit, that I saw anyone but Vikki wear an Icelandic sweater. Our guide mentioned it had become a tourist sell and having browsed a few shops I could guess why.

Icelandic wool isn't the softest. I fingered sweaters and scarves in shops, the wool itchy enough I would hesitate to wear it. It does have benefits other than warmth. Icelandic sheep have a dual coat; a soft undercoat and a coarser outer coat that keeps the sheep warm and protected.[7] That means it has water and wear-resistant properties,

---

5. Chincoteague. *Official Chincoteague Island Pony Swim Guide.* 2023 https://www.chincoteague.com/pony_swim_guide.html

6. Smithsonian Mag. *Iceland's Annual Tradition of Counting Sheep Is Far From Sleepy.* Laura Kiniry. Oct, 2022. https://www.smithsonianmag.com/travel/icelands-annual-tradition-of-counting-sheep-is-far-from-sleepy-180981038/

7. Icelandic Sheep Breeders of North America. *About Icelandic Sheep.* 2023 https://www.isbona.com/index.php/about-icelandic-sheep

which can do wonders for the life of a sweater. The wool is also considered one of the best for felting. [8]

From the triplet craters, we headed to another hot spring. While both the Blue Lagoon and the Mývatn baths are natural hot springs in that the water is geothermically heated, neither of the spas would exist without human involvement. The water they use is cast away from geothermal power plants and is cooled to a human-safe temperature before filling constructed spas.

What we saw before lunch was hot water bubbling out of the ground, in transparent pillars no larger than an inch and a half. Warnings around the area declared the water above boiling temperature, and the heat in the air was wonderful, chasing away any chill from the day. With the heat came steam, extreme enough that my glasses fogged constantly. I couldn't help sticking my face into though, it felt like a spa treatment. I'm grateful for the railing making sure I stayed just over an arm's length away from the string of springs. I wouldn't have been able to see how far away I was otherwise and probably would have stuck my hand in hot water on accident.

While a wonder, the spring was tiny. Maybe twenty steps across. Only Mom took any photos, and all you can see is a curtain of steam rising from the dip in the ground between a hill and the walkway where the little jets of water splashed.

---

8. Elkhorn Icelandic Sheep. *Fleece & Fiber Quality*. 2016 https://www.icelandicsheep.com/resources/quick-facts-about-icelandic-sheep/fleece-and-fiber-quality/

Lava Falls

After a morning of less famous sites, we headed to Hraunfossar, or 'Lava Falls'. Its beauty and proximity to Reykjavik have made it a common stop on many day tours that head north of the city.

Hraunfossar isn't a flood of water diving over a cliff side, but a series of short cascades flowing gently into a river with a milky blue color. The water seeps out of lava rock and flows from rivulets traveling across a nearby lava field before falling the short distance.[1]

While Goðafoss had stolen my heart, this one stole my mom's. "It's so gentle," she said, looking over the whole range stretching nearly 3,000 ft along the river. There was no roar, no spray kicked up by the water entering the river. Just a white noise level of sound that would be easy to fall asleep to. There wasn't even bird song.

We linked arms, heading up the trail to another waterfall – Barnafoss, or Children's Waterfall.

---

1. Wikipedia. *Hraunfossar.* 2023 https://en.wikipedia.org/wiki/Hraunfossar

Barnafoss is not very tall either, but it's messy and churns. You can't see the water fall so much as you see it froth in pools of different heights, the descent hidden by rocks. The waterfall got its name from a story about a pair of children.[2] Their mother had gone to Christmas service, leaving her children behind, and when she returned they were gone. Searchers found child footprints leading to a stone arch over the river, but nothing on the other side.

The story says the mother, in her grief, had the bridge destroyed to prevent a similar incident, but today you can see a small arch over the white froth of the river. A new one carved by the water, or a different, untraversable one as described in the story, I'm not sure. In either case, even from hundreds of feet away, the water looked dangerous.

The waterfalls were our lunch stop, allowing us to enjoy the small café on a hill over the river. We couldn't quite see Hraunfossar from inside the building, it sat too low, but it was nice to have enough time at a site to do all that we wanted. See the sights. Eat an unhurried lunch. And spend five minutes browsing a rather pitiful gift corner.

I'd started to feel like Mom, wondering if I'd ever have the shopping time to get a small item or two as a reminder. It became a bigger concern when we learned our expected arrival at the hotel was 5 pm. Stores closed at 6, and our taxi pickup the next day was when stores would just be opening. I would have less than an hour to get a souvenir, assuming of course I could figure out *what* I wanted.

---

2. Guide to Iceland. *A Day Trip to Waterfalls in West Iceland.* Jorunn. 2023 https://guidetoiceland.is/connect-with-locals/jorunnsg/a-little-daytrip-direction-west-iceland

Snorri Sturluson

We headed to what our guide called a historical center, but what might be more accurate to call a minuscule village with a huge history. Reykholt only has 60 inhabitants, but in the 13th century, it'd been home to Snorri Sturluson.[1] In the village there's a statue of him, the ruins of his home, and a small museum.

I'd never heard of Sturluson, but I had heard of his works - Prose Edda and Heimskringla. Prose Edda is considered the Norse version of the Odyssey. It's the first written account of Old Norse mythology and is very, very thick. In gift shops, I'd seen paperbacks over 1,000 words. [2] Prior to Sturluson's work, the stories had only been told orally.

---

1. Wikipedia. *Reykholt, Western Iceland.* 2022 https://en.wikipedia.org/wiki/Reykholt,_Western_Iceland

2. Guide to Iceland. *Reykholt Travel Guide.* 2023 https://guidetoiceland.is/travel-iceland/drive/reykholt

I'd considered buying a copy as it's considered the fullest, most detailed source of Norse myths, [3] until I flipped through a copy. The prose was thick and clunky, the norm I'd say for medieval translated text. I've read Neil Gaiman's Norse Mythology which was much more accessible, but I wouldn't say no to reading a modernized version of the Prose Edda.

I would be willing to give the Poetic Edda a try. It's an even older collection of stories in the form of poems [4] and had been a source for Sturluson's Prose Edda. However, I have tried and failed to read epic poetry from the 17th century a few years ago. I imagine it'd be a larger struggle to read something from the 13th.

Sturluson's other work, Heimskringla, is a saga depicting the history of Swedish and Norwegian kings.[5] I have little desire to read this one. It's not that I don't understand or value history, but it usually only calls to me if I have a connection to the subject. I'm much more interested in the mythologies of cultures and countries, which I pin on my Greek heritage.

Greek myths were everywhere when I was a child, taught in school and inspiring all sorts of media. It was an easily accessed connection to my mom's culture, and from there I jumped from one culture to another – Welsh, Celtic, Egyptian, Germanic, Japanese. I like looking at the patterns between them, like how animal brides are found in Europe, Africa, and Asia. I track how they are interrupted

---

3. Wikipedia. *Prose Edda*. 2023 https://en.wikipedia.org/wiki/Prose_Edda

4. Wikipedia. *Poetic Edda*. 2023 https://en.wikipedia.org/wiki/Poetic_Edda

5. Wikipedia. *Heimskringla*. 2023 https://en.wikipedia.org/wiki/Heimskringla

in different ways, like how Arthurian myths got more and more romantic, or the recent trend of fairytale retellings in YA literature. I like contrasting them too, comparing the Irish fae to the American version that steals teeth.

Snorri Sturluson, however, was a straight historian, compiling accounts with little analysis. When not writing history, Sturluson was involved in politics. He was a member of Iceland's Parliament, and some believed he was a lackey of the Norwegian king. He wasn't well-liked in his time, having a hand in prodding Iceland to civil war and causing chaos. Nearly everyone he knew betrayed him and he was ultimately assassinated. It's this fact alone that's turned him into a national hero. Assassination was such a taboo in Iceland that his cause of death propelled him into martyrdom. Instead of a legacy of causing trouble, his works have garnered international attention.

Our guide called his history a real-life Game of Thrones situation. I believe it.

Reykholt is home to a museum and library focused on Sturluson's work and other medieval literature. [6] There's not much left of Sturluson's home, just low rows of rock that outline what used to be a house and hints of a collapsed tunnel between the ruins and a spring, thought to be where Sturluson bathed. Michele stuck her hand in the water and wrinkled her nose. Maybe the circle of water had been warmed in the 13th century, but any access to geothermal heat had long since moved away.

---

6. Snorrastofa. *Library*. 2023 https://www.snorrastofa.is/en/snorrastofa/bokhlada

Despite the museum being the main attraction in Reykholt, none of us saw an exhibit. Instead, the entire bus milled around the gift shop. With many of us having flights leaving the next day, everyone was looking for something.

Mom found herself attracted to the jewelry display. She's always liked jewelry, rings especially, and while art is my typical souvenir, adornments are hers. Our last international trip, she's gotten two necklaces – an orthodox cross with rubies and an evil eye necklace. The first was for her, the latter was because there was a set of three and she decided that would be a perfect Christmas gift for me, her, and my sister who'd also joined us on that trip to Greece.

Mom tried on ring after ring, chatting with Vikki about designs and styles. I don't care for rings; I do too much with my hands – typing, crafting – but I love earrings and necklaces. There were a few in the shop that were passable, but nothing I liked enough to pull out my wallet for. I was, however, reminded of a necklace I'd seen in Reykjavik on our first day.

Michele and I caught each other's eyes, shaking our heads fondly at Vikki and Mom. They were the shoppers in the group, whereas she and I were content with the books we'd gotten in Akureyri. We explored the grounds a little bit; there was a horse paddock several of us hung around hoping to pet the horse. When it came time to board the bus, our guide asked me to see if I could hurry my mother along. We had a time limit, after all.

It took a few minutes to rush Mom into her purchase – she had to make a final selection, then I had to run to the bus to get her purse, and then she had to pay and collect the paperwork to get the VAT refund. I rolled my eyes and suffered a light slap from Vikki, but I didn't mind. Shopping makes my mom happy, and she proudly showed off her ring on the bus.

She looked as pleased as punch a few months later when I opened a Christmas gift. That ask to have me get her purse had been a ruse – she'd bought a pair of earrings that matched her ring for me.

Sturlureyki Horse Farm

Our last attraction of a tour – the Sturlureyki horse farm - sadly had no sheep for Vikki, but they had two stables full of Icelandic horses.

As a breed, the Icelandic horse is short and stocky. They're not ponies, as ponies are technically a separate species, but I have seen ponies as tall as these creatures. I showed horses for my high school team, and my first summer job was working on Mackinac Island for the carriage tour company where I regularly dealt with draft horses. The contrast to the short stature of these animals, whose shoulders were lower than mine, was stark. I wondered how it would feel to sit on one. Would my feet hang below their bellies?

Riding was out of the question, but we got plenty of opportunities to pet the horses and feed them treats as we got a tour of the farm. The Sturlureyki farm was the first location to use a geothermal heating system in Europe. Built in 1907, it pipes water from a hot spring on the farm into the stables and farmhouse to keep them warm.[1]

The farm also uses geothermal heat to bake, just like early Icelandic settlers. The farm hands showed us a dug-out oven lined with hard clay. I was surprised by how small the oven was, I'd been imagining them the size of a pizza oven. But in reality, it was more like a Dutch oven on its side. Inside, two aluminum foil-wrapped loaves were pressed tight against each other.

"How do you know if they're done?" Michele asked.

The farm hand shrugged. "They're just done." They didn't time the baking, but it took a day per loaf. Whether that was twenty-two hours or twenty-four didn't matter so much. We got to sample one of the loaves. Like what we had during our food tour on day one, it was dense and brown, but it lacked the same sweetness. This recipe lacked molasses.

As we nibbled on the bread, the staff talked to us about the Icelandic horse. Iceland is very protective of them, to the point where the European farm hands – college students on a gap year – hadn't been allowed to bring their gear due to concerns of bringing over a disease. There are so few native diseases, that there's a worry the breed has no defense against an abroad variant. Part of this comes from how isolated the breed is – Icelandic law prohibits horses from being imported into the country and any horses that leave cannot return.[2] While such regulations mitigate any outbreaks at stables, it

---

1. Sturlureykir Horse Farm. *Stable Visit.* 2023 https://sturlureykirhorses.is/stable-visit/

also means the Icelandic horse is one of the purest in the world with a limited amount of crossbreed offspring.

In the horse world, what makes the Icelandic Horse stand out is how it moves.

Most breeds have four gaits – walk, trot, canter, and gallop. Each is identified by a particular pattern of footwork around how hooves hit the ground before the pattern repeats. Walk is a four-beat gait and each leg moves separately: left hind, left fore, right hind, right fore. Trot is a two-beat gait, the legs move in pairs on the diagonal: the left hind and right foreleg move together. Canter is a more complicated three-beat gait, with one set of legs working together. The horse pushes itself forward with a single hind leg, hitting the ground first with a diagonal set of legs before the second foreleg lands, and then using that original rear leg to propel the next step forward. Gallops are full-out runs and only slightly differ from canters – instead of the second beat being a diagonal pair of legs hitting the ground, the rear leg hits first. There's no switch off between the front and rear legs - the back two hit the ground, and then the front two.[3] Both canters and gallops have moments of suspension – no feet on the ground.

The Icelandic horse has extra gaits.[4]

The first is the tölt. It's a four-beat gait, so each foot hits the ground separately. Whereas in a walk propulsion comes from all legs, in a tölt, the horse propels itself forward using its hind legs. It's very showy because the extra work the back legs do allows the forelegs to snap

---

3. Wikipedia. *Horse gait*. 2023 https://en.wikipedia.org/wiki/Horse_gait

4. Horses of Iceland. *The Five Gaits*. 2023 https://www.horsesoficeland.is/the-icelandic-horse-gaits

up and curl. The other unique gait is the flying pace, which contains elements of a canter but is a two-beat gait like a trot. The diagonal legs move together, but the horse is moving with enough power it enters suspension.

I've never ridden at a gallop, but I've done walks, trots, and canters aplenty. I'd love to try a tölt or flying pace. They're moving gaits, so you can go quite fast, but they're also touted to be very smooth. Trots are so bouncy they can be annoying, and you usually move up and down in the saddle to the beat or stay standing to prevent your boobs from jiggling. I can't imagine what the flying pace feels like in the saddle, with the same pattern but lacking a jolt.

As always when I'm near horses, Mom gets excited and needs photos of me with them. I used to be a very invested horse girl, with a collection of nearly a hundred models, insisted on a horse wallpaper for my bedroom, and used to eat grass. My kid brain thought grass was essential to a horse's speed and I wanted to run like the wind as well. I was around them regularly in my late teens between weekly lessons, the high school equestrian team, and summer jobs. I see horses and remember hanging out in the barn with friends or helping teammates with show makeup. My mom remembers late nights polishing leather and 4 am drives with me napping in the passenger seat.

Standing next to one of the horses, my hand on the lead line, I felt like I lost fifteen years. I stroked the horse's neck and gave her a whole handful of treats. I'm sure all the horses there are spoiled.

Eventually, it was time to go and the reality of the end of the trip hit us.

Our guide dropped us off at our hotels one by one, each person leaving to a course of goodbyes and waves and well wishes for the return home. It was impossible not to have a fondness for each of our bus mates after spending six days in each other's company, and the tour Whatsapp group still exists. It's not my most active chat, but our guide did share photos of his newborn we all cooed over.

Hallgrímskirkja

I'd set my mind on a very specific souvenir as the day progressed. An oval lava stone pendant, divided by a vertical gold setting, strung on a gold chain.

"I got thirty minutes to get to a jewelry store before it closes," I told the group after dumping my suitcase on a table. "So I'm heading out now because I don't want to miss my window."

I'd never seen my mom get ready so fast, but she was not letting me go shopping without her.

We left together, me leading the way with my long strides. I learned enough of Reykjavik's layout in the few days we'd spent downtown I was confident I could navigate to the store, but I didn't know the store's name or distance from the hotel. I guided us based on city landmarks, my memory, and a look at Google Maps before we left. While I took the direct route, heading south until we hit the cross street, the street was a diagonal one and it's possible a different route would have saved us, if not time, a hill climb.

Vikki and Michele begged a break from my pace, splitting off into a coffee shop, while Mom continued the powerwalk with me. We hit the store with ten minutes to spare. I walked through the door, and Mom trucked on past me. We'd hit an area of the city she remembered, and she wanted to pop into a different store.

There was someone already in the store and their discussion with the cashier carried on long enough that Michele, Vikki, and Mom reconvened in my shop before I could make my purchase. Vikki fingered a few earrings, contemplating a pair, while Michele enjoyed looking at the small collection of fancy hats. She offered me a piece of a cookie, and the four of us finished it while the cashier got together my paperwork for the VAT refund.

Sometimes it truly is better to get fine jewelry abroad. The exchange rate is often in favor of the American dollar, and tax is typically refunded by customs. Jewelry bought, we headed toward the one Reykjavik attraction we'd wanted to visit but hadn't yet: Hallgrímskirkja.

Hallgrímskirkja is a hard-to-miss symbol of Reykjavik. Its location is a big part of that – it sits at the top of a hill, with the main street leading from it a prominent shopping and dining location. The other is that it looks like a rocket ship. From the west, the front of the grey stone building climbs the sky and two wings extend to either side in a curved slope. Quite a design for a church.

Guðjón Samúelsson designed the Lutheran church in 1937.[1] At the time he was the State Architect of Iceland, a title I'm just tickled

---

1. Adventures. *A Complete Guide to Hallgrimskirkja Church*. 2023 https://adventures.com/iceland/attractions/museums-churches/hallgrimskirkja-church/

that exists. He was also Iceland's first trained architect and was a contemporary of Frank Lloyd Wright. As far as I'm aware, they'd never met, but both men were practicing architects from the 1920s to 1950s and aimed to create a style of architecture unique to their countries. Wright developed Prairie Style, inspired by the landscape of Illinois, featuring flat, open homes with straight, horizontal lines.[2] Samúelsson never named his style, but he was heavily inspired by the hexagonal basalt columns that fill the country's landscape. Hallgrímskirkja's curved wings mimic them, constructed of columns of decreasing height. Grouped columns of various heights edge the body of the church, matched by their twins inside the modernist nave and at the end of each set of pews.

Inside Hallgrímskirkja resides the largest pipe organ I've ever seen. 50 ft tall, it weighs 25 tons and contains 5,275 pipes. The largest is 31 ft tall. It's in use today, and I can only imagine how it sounds echoing in the church, the high domes capturing and sending back each note. Both times I've been to Iceland haven't coincided with a concert, so that's another thing I might insist on for a future trip.

The needle of its rocket shape is the bell tower, stretching 240 ft tall. The elevator to the top is a tiny thing that shakes, barely fitting six people, and it deposits you in a tight stone room. Along the walls were a series of floor-to-ceiling panels detailing religion in Iceland as well as the church's namesake - Hallgrímur Pétursson. Pétursson was

---

2. Wikipedia. *Frank Lloyd Wright. Prairie Style Houses (1900-1914).* 2023 https://en.wikipedia.org/wiki/Frank_Lloyd_Wright#Prairie_Style_houses_(1900%E2%80%931914)

a Lutheran priest and poet known for writing the Passion Hymns.[3] Each of the 50 hymns explores the Passion of Christ, and it's sung or read in Iceland every Lent. They're not well-sung or read outside of Iceland, but have been translated into several languages.

While reading through the small exhibit, the bells rang. I was a short flight of stairs below, so I bolted up the steps into the belfry. I opened the door to the covered, but open top floor just as the last note faded. Vikki and Michele, who'd been there when they rang, slowly uncovered their ears and relaxed the wince on their faces.

"Ow," a kid in the tower said, their mom laughing.

Maybe it had been a good thing I missed the bells.

Looking up, I could see the carillon of 29 bells and three solo bells.[4] I thought about witnessing the next performance, but between the cold air from standing in the tallest spot in Reykjavik and Vikki's warning about saving my eardrums, I descended before the next quarter-hour bell.

I looked out each window of the tower before going downstairs. There are eight, two in each direction, and on clear days you can see miles. Reykjavik's brightly colored buildings. Mountains near and far. The harbor, and beyond that the ocean.

It's painfully obvious from up there how small Reykjavik is. I'm from Chicago; I've stood on the observation decks of the John Han-

---

3. Wikipedia. *Passion Hymns*. 2022 https://en.wikipedia.org/wiki/Passion_Hymns

4. Reykjavik Grapevine. *Finally The Church Bells Of Hallgrímskirkja Will Toll Once Again*. Elias Torsson. Oct 2017 https://grapevine.is/news/2017/10/23/finally-the-church-bells-of-hallgrimskirkja-will-toll-once-again/

cock and Sears Tower and if you look west or north you can't see the edge of the city. But from Hallgrímskirkja, you can see the entirety of Iceland's capital. It's compact, easy to navigate, but so full of small unique museums it would take days to see them all and weeks to try all the restaurants that caught my eye. Small isn't always bad, it's why I live in the suburbs rather than West Loop, and it's nice to know you can capture Reykjavik's charming nature in a single shot.

It had been a souvenir from my last trip – a watercolor canvas print of this very view from Hallgrímskirkja.

"Ready to go?" Mom asked. Leave Iceland? No. But leave the church and go to dinner? Yeah.

Reykjavik Night Life

Mom spotted a restaurant our food guide recommended, and we headed inside. I immediately felt underdressed. The hostess was in all black, the lights were low, and here we were in the clothes we'd dressed in for hikes and worn to the horse farm.

This was a restaurant for anniversary dates, not tired, hungry hikers. Vikki and I shot each other uncomfortable looks, but Michele walked right up to the hostess and put our names in for a table. To her credit, or perhaps she's used to tourists after a long day coming in, the hostess took her name and that was that.

We elected to wait at the bar, rounding the corner and getting a face full of the restaurant's theme – the roaring 20s. The Gilded Age. Brass and copper gleamed everywhere, and facing the bar were low, plush velvet booths. Fake plants hung from the ceiling, and next to the bar was an old train car, 'The Champagne Train' painted above the windows.

Mom immediately stepped in, touching the tufted booths and the historical wallpaper. Champagne is her favorite thing to drink. "Take a picture" she called out, standing in the opening of the train.

I did, of course, and she had the largest smile on her face.

One of the reasons I love traveling with my mom is the joy she finds in the simplest, silliest things. Just like she'd picked up a large chunk of ice at Glacier Lagoon to pretend it was a tiara, here she was having fun. It's a shock sometimes, not because she's never happy, but because when I was younger I expected to grow out of focused joy. Kids get excited to see a doll of their favorite character, or when the dino exhibit at the zoo includes their favorite carnivore. As you get older, you're supposed to get more serious. Yes, you're happy and can have fun, but it's not over random things or playing pretend.

My mom indulged my hyperfocuses and favorite things when I was a child, but as I got older I realized I could indulge myself. I'm an adult! I have money! I can buy a mermaid costume if I want to and make a mermaid bathroom. I buy matching jewelry for me and my mom! I can raise my leg and shadow kick Michele's shadow, starting a shadow war on the top of a mountain! I can have a slumber party at Vikki's!

Things I expected to be cringe later in life, that I would be embarrassed to like or embarrassed to express a like for, have never materialized and I credit a lot of that to my mom. She was enthusiastic to see a fake train car dedicated to her favorite drink. Loved the experience of sitting on the old booths and sipping a champagne cocktail as we pretended to be on a trip. People say all the time that aging doesn't mean growing old or growing up, but my mom embodies that in a way that doesn't make me fear aging.

"Your mom is so cool," Vikki has told me multiple times, but it's different than the cool of high school parents who give you the independence to go to parties, drink, or stay up late. It's the type of cool that you admire.

Mom's always happy about something. Always sees something cool or special or joyful.

I want to be the same way when I'm in my sixties.

Drinks morphed into dinner, with prices so outrageous we thought about leaving. But as Michele said, it was our last night. It felt right to do something special. And really, what was a $90 tasting menu to the thousands we spent on the trip? Still, we split two tasting menus and an appetizer, allowing us to select different dishes to sample. One by one, our waitress brought out plates of amazing food. We took small bites, sharing everything between us. From the fish to the sauce to the vegetables, everything was delicious.

We left the restaurant satisfied, but not ready to head back to the hotel. It was our last night! The desire to linger in the streets was strong and we went searching for a cocktail bar. We came across a bookstore that had a bar *and* a stage for live music called Mál Og Menning[1].

I went straight to the bar, ordering cocktails and a dessert to share, while Michele and Vikki headed up the stairs to find a table. I love bookstores that have cafes, but this place went above and beyond

---

1. Iceland Review. *Mál og menning Bookstore Starts a New Chapter*. Larissa Kyzer. Oct 2020 https://www.icelandreview.com/business/mal-og-menning-bookstore-starts-a-new-chapter/

with three full shelves of liquor and a specialty cocktail menu in addition to snacks.

As I waited for my slice of cake, I watched the band in the center of the store. There was a small stage, surrounded by seats in a cleared-out center. The four-piece band performed covers of older American pop numbers, and I carried dessert up the stairs while nodding to the beat.

Vikki and Michele had no trouble finding a free table, and we settled into the vibe of the place. From the second story we couldn't see the band, but music drifted up and the wide windows let us look out onto Reykjavik's nightlife. We'd come at the right time because as we finished the cake, the band played their last song and staff circled to announce closing.

We drained our drinks and made our way outside, eager for a bar. We walked down the main drag, which wasn't very crowded or brightly lit, hoping to find an open place to drink. Sadly, our finds were murals and shopping displays. Nightlife was scarce past 11 pm. We resigned ourselves to walking down Laugavegur for the last time, passing by our hotel from the first few nights, until we turned down a side street to return to our beds.

Sleep couldn't claim us yet. We pulled out receipts and paperwork to get our VAT refunds at the airport, packed our bags, and confirmed our taxi pickup. I was proud of myself for having little Icelandic currency left thanks to spending most of it on my new necklace, while Mom dithered about, hoping to have a chance to spend hers at the airport.

Eventually, we settled in our beds with alarms set. The taxi would come at 9 am, and we wanted to have the time for a good, hearty breakfast.

Departure

I woke up our last day ready to go, mind full of things to do. Pack my pajamas, brush my teeth and pack the toothpaste, make sure everything I needed for the airport was accessible, and screenshot my boarding pass.

It had been a weird night, if only because I hadn't shared a bed with Vikki. Our other hotels had pressed the double beds together to form a queen, but this one kept the mattresses separate so we slept a foot apart. We'd never crossed over into each other's space the whole trip, so I knew the mattress was wide enough, but I'd spent the night aware of both the right and left edges where before I'd only worried about one.

Crammed into one suite, all four of us shared a bathroom. We went in and out regularly as we got ready, using the mirror above the desk instead of the sink to do our hair. I pressed down my clothes, collected all the receipts, and checked every nightstand for left behind small items.

Vikki was the late one, still doing her morning routine as Mom, Michele, and I went down to breakfast. I helped myself to skyr, sure I'd never find the sour yogurt in the States for a price I'd want to pay, and the mini croissants. With a noon take-off, was United expecting us to eat before we boarded? We'd land roughly 6 pm Chicago time, was that too soon for dinner? Not knowing what, or if, I'd be fed on the plane I made sure to eat a breakfast and a half.

"It's the last day," Vikki sobbed as she joined us.

"One last picture then," Michele said. She positioned us around a table, snapping a selfie of us in the hotel dining area.

"I'm gonna miss you ladies," Vikki said. "I'm so glad we took this trip together."

I smiled, looking around the table. It really was amazing how well we traveled as a unit, and it would be fabulous to do a future trip. I'd see all of these women again in the future, but I couldn't think of a reason why we'd all be in a room together. Not unless it was another joint vacation.

"We'll plan another one," Mom said, as Michele started listing off places.

Like our departure to Iceland was well timed, our departure to the States also worked seamlessly. We rolled our suitcases into the lobby as our taxi arrived, and we ooo'd over the Tesla Model Y. Mom's face lit up at the car, already in shopping mode. She'd started the slow process of looking for a new car, and how roomy the backseat was with three adult women impressed her. There was plenty of elbow and ankle space.

"Should I put it through its paces?" the driver asked.

"You betcha!" Mom said and he zoomed up a hill to get us out of the city.

We talked with our driver for the hour to the airport, mainly about our trip and what we'd seen. The concept of *next time* was on everyone's tongue. Michele wanted to bring her husband. Mom wanted to bring Dad. Vikki had found a sheep ranch you could stay at.

I laughed. "I love how we're all already planning our next trips here."

"It's a beautiful country," the driver said.

I don't usually do repeats. I rarely reread books. Or rewatch movies or shows. I've been to Greece and Germany twice, mainly because I have family in both, but always made sure to have a different itinerary. Will I ever return to Ethiopia? Who knows. London or Belgium or Ecuador or New Zealand or Denver or Albuquerque or New Orleans? No clue. But I'm 100% confident that I'll return to Iceland.

Part of that is how close it is to Chicago. A six-hour flight is very doable, and tickets aren't that bad for an international flight. It's a small country, so it's easy to see a lot of things in a short amount of time. But the main reason for my return is that every time I visit, I find spectacular views.

My first trip introduced me to the area around Reykjavik. My second to the beauty of the east and north sides of the island. What I want to do next is find the time to linger. A multi-day hiking trip. Rent a car and do the ring road at my own pace so I can stare at a waterfall for an hour if I want. Lay in the grass somewhere and nap in the sun, hoping a sheep edges closer. See the Northern Lights in January, when the activity is higher. Look at the ocean during the long, extended sunsets as the time of the midnight sun approaches.

Yes, there are museums I haven't seen in Iceland yet. Horses I haven't ridden, ruins to explore. But it's the waterfalls that will bring me back. The hypnotic roar as they fall into picturesque gorges. The way the rivers they feed snake through hills on their way to the ocean. It's the fresh air, the fantasy landscapes. The dedication of the country to nature and slow living.

You can't *not* love Iceland, and once there, the country will never let you go.

Iceland Guide

While this book isn't a guidebook, I wanted to include a list of recommendations.

Things to Do and See is a list of activities I enjoyed. Some links will take you to tour options, some won't, but as a starting place for booking activities I'd recommend the tour group I went with – Arctic Adventures – or the aggregator site Guide to Iceland.

Places to Eat is focused on the capital, as once we left Reykjavik options dropped dramatically and we often ate a location because it was the only one.

Places to Stay lists all the hotels we stayed at around the country, in Reykjavik and on the ring road. The beauty of booking a tour meant that Arctic Adventures handled lodging, which can be a pain to search for. Like I mentioned in the book, hotels are very scattered so trying to find one on the route can be difficult. Even if you plan on driving yourself around the island, I recommend booking a self-guided tour that includes an itinerary, car, and lodging plan. I've done road trips in America where you drive until you're tired and then stay at a place you see off the highway. That *will not work* in Iceland.

Things to Do and See

- Reykjavik Food Lover's Tour: Icelandic Traditional Food offered by Your Friend In Reykjavik

    - Visited a variety of places in the capital, all delicious. Arrive hungry!

- Reykjavik Maritime Museum

    - A small, but super educational museum on the niche topic of Icelandic fishing.

- Blue Lagoon

    - Iceland's most famous spa, known for its bright blue water and healing properties

- Þingvellir (Thingvellir) National Park

    - Site of the founding of Iceland's parliament and a continental divide

- The Golden Circle

    - A collection of three stops (Þingvellir, Geysir Geothermal Park, Gullfoss waterfall) that's a common day trip from Reykjavik

- Skógafoss

    - An impressive waterfall with a treasure-hunting myth

- Fjaðrárgljúfur Canyon

    - A tucked-away magical river canyon that's been in a Justin Beiber video

- Vatnajökull National Park

    - Iceland's largest national park. Day trips and multi-day hikes galore. Many popular Iceland destinations (Skaftafell, Glacier Lagoon) lie within the park

- Glacier Hike on Falljökull

    - 3-hour hike on the glacier, with wonderful guides.

- Diamond Beach and Glacier Lagoon

    - A lagoon filled with baby icebergs from a nearby glacier and a beach known for the clear ice that washes on shore. My absolute favorite spot.

- Hengifoss

- One of the tallest waterfalls in Iceland, known for the unique rock strata it falls down and the sheep ice cream stand at the hike's end.

- Dettifos

  - A large, powerful waterfall in the NE of Iceland. It's part of the Diamon Circle, a collection of northern features.

- Dimmuborgir

  - A unique lava field seeped in myths like the Yule Lads

- Goðafoss

  - A horseshoe waterfall with historical importance. My favorite of the trip

- Hraunfossar

  - A gentle, long waterfall with a nearby café

- Hallgrímskirkja

  - Lutheran church at the highest point of Reykjavik whose bell tower offers amazing views

Places to Eat in Reykjavik

- Iðnó https://www.instagram.com/idnorvk/
    - A delightful cultural house near Parliament with traditional soup
- 101 Reykjavik Street Food https://101reykjavikstreetfood.is/
    - Icelandic fish-based street food
- Bæjarins Beztu Pylsur https://bbp.is/
    - Reykjavik hot dog stand
- Seabaron https://www.instagram.com/theseabaronrvk/?hl=en
    - Harbor-side seafood restaurant
- Baka Baka https://www.instagram.com/bakabaka_rvk/

- Amazing bakery with items ranging from croissants to bread loaves

- Monkey's https://monkeys.is/en/monkeys-english/

  - Pricey, but delicious and a great place to treat yourself

Places to Stay

- Vintage Hotel https://www.booking.com/hotel/is/townhouse-41.html

- Adventure Hotel Geirland https://www.booking.com/hotel/is/hotel-geirland.html

- Hotel Smyrlabjörg https://smyrlabjorg.is/en/

- Hotel Valaskjalf https://valaskjalf.is/en/

- Berjaya Akureyri Hotel https://www.icelandhotelcollectionbyberjaya.com/en/hotels/north/akureyri-hotel

- Hotel Laugarbakki https://hotellaugarbakki.is/

- Fosshotel Baron https://www.islandshotel.is/hotels-in-iceland/fosshotel-baron/

Please Review

Thank you so much for reading Shores & Falls: Traveling Iceland's Ring Road! If you could do me a favor, please leave a rating or review?

Reviews are extremely important for any book, but for indie books like this they are crucial. Reviews help potential readers discover new books and determine if a book is right for them. They also help authors by increasing exposure, showing the author their work is appreciated, and can serve as a guide to improve future books.

I'd really appreciate it if you took a minute to write a review of this book, be it on Amazon or Goodreads. It doesn't have to be long, maybe tell future readers your favorite part or leave an emoji string. A simple rating can also make a difference.

Reviews are the second-best way to help an independent author (after buying a book).

Virginia Mueller

Virginia 'Ginny' Mueller is a travel fanatic, who loves to take advantage of living near a large international airport. She's lived in three countries, has hit every continent but Antarctica (it's on the list), and loves sharing what she learns on her adventures.

www.ingramcontent.com/pod-product-compliance
Lightning Source LLC
Chambersburg PA
CBHW052141070526
44585CB00017B/1917